DADAR RAILWAY STATION

MARINE DRIVE

LEARNING FROM MUMBAI

LEARNING FROM MUMBAI

PRACTISING ARCHITECTURE IN URBAN INDIA

PELLE POIESZ • GERT JAN SCHOLTE
SANNE VANDERKAAIJ GANDHI

MAPIN PUBLISHING

First published in India in 2013 by
Mapin Publishing Pvt. Ltd
706 Kaivanna, Panchvati, Ellisbridge,
Ahmedabad 380006
T: 91 79 4022 8228 • F: 91 79 4022 8201
E: mapin@mapinpub.com
www.mapinpub.com

The publishers would like to thank the Consulate General of the Kingdom of The Netherlands, Mumbai, for their generous support towards publication of this edition.

Text © Pelle Poiesz, Gert Jan Scholte, Sanne Vanderkaaij Gandhi, Rohan Varma, Charles Correa, and Rahul Mehrotra
Photographs and illustrations © as listed below:
Timo Cents: pp. 42-45, 78, 166
Bas Losekoot: Cover, endpapers, pp. 11, 32, 58, 86, 90–104, 124, 186
Pelle Poiesz and Gert Jan Scholte: pp. 4, 12, 24, 31, 38, 68, 110, 112, 118, 136, 142, 148, 158, 178
Sanne Vanderkaaij Gandhi: p. 163
Paulus Veltman and Anja Brunt: p. 164
All other photographs and illustrations were obtained from the interviewed architects and urbanists.

All rights reserved under international copyright conventions. No part of this book may be reproduced or transmitted in any form or by any means, electronic or mechanical, including photocopy, recording or any other information storage and retrieval system, without prior permission in writing from the publisher.

The moral rights of Pelle Poiesz, Gert Jan Scholte, Sanne Vanderkaaij Gandhi, Rohan Varma, Charles Correa and Rahul Mehrotra as authors of this work are asserted.

ISBN: 978-81-89995-81-2

Concept: Pelle Poiesz and Gert Jan Scholte (mail@learningfrommumbai.nl)
Text of Interviews: Sanne Vanderkaaij Gandhi
Copyediting: David Raats
Design: studio ilse van klei (ilsevanklei.nl)
Production: Mapin Design Studio
Printed by Parksons Graphics, Mumbai

The design workshop 'Learning from Mumbai 2012' at the Sir J.J. College of Architecture received funding from the Consulate General of the Kingdom of The Netherlands, Mumbai, India.

Learning from Mumbai received funding from the **creative industries fund NL**

Endpapers:
Front: View of South Mumbai from the Imperial Twin Towers
Back: View of Belassis Rd. from the Imperial Twin Towers

ONGC OFFICE BUILDING BY ARCHITECT HAFEEZ CONTRACTOR, BANDRA KURLA COMPLEX

CONTENTS

PREFACE
Pelle Poiesz, Gert Jan Scholte and Sanne Vanderkaaij Gandhi 8

ARTICLES

THE MAKING OF THE MAXIMUM CITY
Rohan Varma 16

PUBLIC TRANSPORT AS DNA
Charles Correa 26

REMAKING MUMBAI
Rahul Mehrotra 34

FACTS AND FIGURES
Timo Cents 40

INTERVIEWS

APPRECIATING THE UNCONTROLLED AND THE UNEXPECTED
Steven Beunder 48

EVERY BUILDING MUST SHOUT
Hafeez Contractor 60

HOUSING 100,000 PEOPLE AT A TIME
Deodhar Associates 70

ORGANIC FARMING IN THE CONCRETE JUNGLE
Adrienne Thadani 80

A NEW LIGHT ON MUMBAI
Bas Losekoot 88

ARCHITECTURE EDUCATION AS A KEY TO APPROPRIATE DEVELOPMENT
Rajiv Mishra 106

INSTILLING A PASSION FOR ARCHITECTURE
Abhijit Mandrekar 114

THE NEXT GENERATION
Mumbai's Young Architects 120

FROM THE NETHERLANDS TO INDIA... AND BEYOND
Shyam Khandekar 126

ACTIVISM AND ARCHITECTURE
PK Das 138

THE ARCHITECT AS A GUARDIAN OF THE PUBLIC REALM
Brinda Somaya 150

THE CITY IS YOUR CANVAS
The Wall Project 160

SOCIALLY AND ENVIRONMENTALLY CONSCIOUS ARCHITECTURE
Robert Verrijt and Shefali Balwani 168

FROM QUANTITY TO QUALITY
Ravi Sarangan 180

ACKNOWLEDGEMENTS
Pelle Poiesz and Gert Jan Scholte 188

PREFACE

PELLE POIESZ
GERT JAN SCHOLTE
SANNE VANDERKAAIJ GANDHI

Pelle Poiesz (1971) was born in Dar es Salaam, Tanzania. He studied at Delft University of Technology (TU Delft) in the Netherlands and at the Sir J.J. College of Architecture in Mumbai. In 2000, together with Manou Huijbregts, he established the architectural firm *HP architecten* in Rotterdam (www.hparchitecten.nl). *HP architecten* is an all-round architectural office with a portfolio that ranges from housing, office, cultural and educational buildings, to fully detailed interior design. The office operates on the central premise that good design creates spaces in which the user feels welcome and at home, respected and inspired.

Gert Jan Scholte (1970) is an architect who studied at the Faculty of Architecture at TU Delft in the Netherlands and at the Sir J.J. College of Architecture in Mumbai. He is the co-founder of *Cityblob*, an Amsterdam-based architecture, urban planning and real estate development company with a particular focus on railway and underground stations and their surrounding areas. A recently realized project is *CU! Amsterdam*, a large-scale sport, retail and leisure development that is part of the new *Amsterdam Bijlmer Arena* railway station.

Sanne Vanderkaaij Gandhi (1979) completed an MA in (Non Western) History at the University of Groningen and an MSc in Asian Studies at the University of Amsterdam (both in the Netherlands). She is finalizing her PhD thesis in International Development Studies at the University of Amsterdam, and works as a freelance researcher and writer. Sanne is based in Mumbai.

In 1992 and 1993 we – Gert Jan Scholte and Pelle Poiesz – 'met' Bombay for the first time, when we studied Architecture at the Sir J.J. College of Architecture. Two decades later we returned to find that its name change was the smallest of transformations it had undergone while we were away. Mumbai, as the city was now called, had grown into a city of almost twenty million inhabitants. It now hosted 20,000 people on each of its square kilometres of land. In some areas the density had even grown to a staggering 140,000 residents per square kilometre. It was in the middle of the largest construction boom it had ever seen in history. Tremendous challenges faced the city, but we found it inhabited by numerous spirited people who presented intriguing observations on its functioning and inspiring solutions for its future. We decided to stay on and see – together with Sanne Vanderkaaij Gandhi –what we could *learn from Mumbai*.

OUTLINE

This volume consists of three parts: a section with background articles, a section with interviews, and a photo essay.

We open with four articles that together provide an introduction to the historical and contemporary context of architecture and urban planning in Mumbai. *Rohan Varma*, in *The Making of the Maximum City*, traces the city's beginnings as seven separate islands occupied by fishing communities and its subsequent development into the megacity it is today. *Charles Correa*, in *Public Transport as DNA*, explores and explains the importance of public transport for the present shape and functioning of Mumbai. *Rahul Mehrotra*, in *Remaking Mumbai*, shifts the discussion to the future by emphasizing the importance of creative, innovative and perhaps even daring solutions for the redevelopment of former industrial areas in the city, such as the mill lands and the eastern waterfronts. This part of the book is concluded by an overview of some *Facts and Figures* on the city compiled by *Timo Cents*. It is accompanied by an account on the difficulties of obtaining quantitative data on and in Mumbai.

In the next section we present the interviews with practising professionals in Mumbai. During our stay in Mumbai we visited a wide variety of firms. Some are engaged in large-scale planning and construction projects and may have the power to set agendas: *Hafeez Contractor, Deodhar Associates, Edifice Consultants* and *Townland Consultants*. Others stand out in particular for their activist, social and heritage conservation projects: *PK Das* and *Brinda Somaya*. Being Dutch ourselves, we were also eager to learn about the differences and similarities between practising architecture in both countries. We interviewed *Shyam Khandekar, Shefali Balwani, Robert Verrijt* and *Abhijit Mandrekar*, who all have set up a new practice, or an extension of their Dutch practice, in Mumbai.

As Mumbai is a young city - the majority of its population is under the age of 30 - we felt it crucial to include the new generation. We conducted a workshop at the Sir J.J. School of Architecture in the early stages of our project, and talked extensively with its Principal, *Rajiv Mishra*. We also held a focus group discussion with four *Young Architects* on what they think Mumbai could teach us. Further, during our travels in Mumbai we kept encountering fresh projects by young people bringing creativity to the city. We decided to include two of these micro-initiatives that – both in their own special way – aim to make Mumbai a more liveable and beautiful place: *Fresh & Local* (*Adrienne Thadani*) and *The Wall Project*.

Finally, we are proud to present a photo essay by *Bas Losekoot*. The photographs he shot in October 2012 in Mumbai are part of his *Urban Millennium Project*, in which he aims to capture life in the world's largest cities through his lens. His photos (quite literally) put the spotlight on an aspect we architects and planners all too easily overlook while we discuss our projects, stare at maps and do our calculations: the users of the city – its inhabitants.

We hope that the current volume answers the question we raised and raises new questions. We hope it draws you to the city, either physically or mentally, and may give you the urge to know more about it. In sum, we hope that, just like we did, you will feel that you have learned from Mumbai and want to keep *Learning from Mumbai*.

Amsterdam, Rotterdam, Mumbai
May 2013

Pelle Poiesz
Gert Jan Scholte
Sanne Vanderkaaij Gandhi

ELPHINSTONE ROAD, FORT

VIEW OF CHOWPATTY BEACH FROM THE HANGING GARDENS

ARTICLES

ARTICLES
ARTICLES
ARTICLES
ARTICLES
ARTICLES
ARTICLES
ARTICLES
ARTICLES
ARTICLES
ARTICLES
ARTICLES
ARTICLES

MUMBAI: THE MAKING OF THE MAXIMUM CITY

ROHAN VARMA

Rohan Varma (1986) graduated as an architect from the Kamla Raheja Vidyanidhi Institute for Architecture and Environmental Studies (KRVIA) at the University of Mumbai in 2009. After graduation, he worked with *Charles Correa Associates* in Mumbai for two years, and then taught for a year at KRVIA. He is a 2011 JN Tata and KC Mahindra Scholar, and is currently pursuing a Master's degree in Architecture and Urbanism at the TU Delft in the Netherlands.

On the shores of the Arabian Sea lies the jewel in India's crown – the city where India meets the world. Mumbai (formerly known as Bombay) was once nothing more than a scattered collection of seven islands off the west coast of India. Over the years the islands were merged by the British to create a city that would one day become the financial capital of India. However, Mumbai is not only India's economic powerhouse, producing almost 40 percent of the country's income tax revenues,[1] but also an urban agglomeration of almost 20.7 million people,[2] which is predicted to grow to an even more astounding 33 million by the year 2025.[3] What sets Mumbai really apart from other megacities are its incredible population densities. The Mumbai Metropolitan Region accommodates more people than the entire nation of the Netherlands, in hardly one-tenth of the area. With a population that has grown almost fivefold in the last fifty years, and restricted by its physical geography as an island city bound by water, densities in many parts of Mumbai average more than 30,000 people per square kilometre[4] – far higher rates than those found in New York, São Paulo or Tokyo.

Mumbai is much more than just its numbers, however. While facts and figures of this 'Maximum City'[5] never fail to baffle, they do little to explain why Mumbai – in spite of its many shortcomings – still remains the *Urbs Prima in Indis* (the First City of India). It is a city that is rich, yet unimaginably poor, chaotic, yet inherently structured, beautiful, yet appalling. But more than anything else, it is India's biggest melting pot and absorber of distress migration, with almost half its population coming from other parts of India.[6] As eminent Indian architect Charles Correa has written: 'Too often we look at our cities from our own self-centred point of view. So we see only the shortages, the failures. But for millions and millions of migrants, landless labourers and wretched have-nots of our society, cities (such as Mumbai) are perhaps their only hope, their only gateway to a better future.'[7]

That has been the very essence of Mumbai from the beginning. More than any other Indian city, Mumbai can stake claim to the title of being a 'City of Opportunities' (a reputation reinforced by the reach of its homemade 'Bollywood' movies). But as Mumbai continues to grow, attracting thousands of migrants each year, it is important to note that it was never expected to become the megacity it is today. As renowned Indian architect Rahul Mehrotra has pointed out, Mumbai, unlike other cities such as New Delhi or Chandigarh, has never been a product of a single preconceived plan.[8] Instead, it has grown over time through a series of planned and unplanned interventions, giving Mumbai its diverse urban fabric and multiple identities. While this has allowed the city to respond to changing contexts, the lack of holistic planning has also led to a city that is now struggling to accommodate its growing population.

Today, more than 55 percent of Mumbai's population lives in informal settlements, and over 65 percent of its workforce is employed in the informal sector[9] (alarming statistics when you consider that Mumbai boasts of being India's richest city). While these may seem recent phenomena, they are in fact products of several complex social, political, and economic events that have taken place during the city's three main periods: those of colonization, modernization, and globalization. What we see today is the physical layering of all those events, making the city in many ways a collage, an assemblage of incredibly diverse fragments, differentiated by religion, community and wealth, all coalesced to form one city: Mumbai.

1 CHAUDHARY, A (2007). *Mumbai, Lagging Shanghai, Faces First Power Cuts in a Century.* Available: http://www.bloomberg.com/apps/news?pid=newsarchive&sid=aAfDo42n1Q3k

2 CENSUS INDIA (2011). Available: http:// www.censusindia.gov.in/2011-prov-results/paper2/data_files/India2/Table_2_PR_Cities_1Lakh_and_Above.pdf. Last accessed 20 October 2012.

3 DAVIS, M (2007). *Planet of Slums.* New York: Verso. 5.

4 BURDETT, R & SUDJIC, D (2011). *Living in the Endless City.* London: Phaidon Press.

5 A REFERENCE TO SUKETU MEHTA'S 2004 BOOK *Maximum City: Bombay Lost and Found.*

6 SINGH, DP (2005). *Migration and Occupation in Mumbai: Issues and Implications.* Mumbai: Tata Institute of Social Sciences. 1 (1), 1-2.

7 CORREA, C (2010). *A Place in the Shade.* Mumbai: Penguin India. 125.

8 MEHROTRA, R (1991). Bombay City - *One Space Two Worlds.* Architecture + Design. 12.

9 BURDETT, R & SUDJIC, D (2011). *Living in the Endless City.* London: Phaidon Press.

COLONIZATION: THE BIRTH OF THE 'DUAL CITY'

Mumbai is first and foremost a 'City on the Water'.[10] Like most other great cities, its close proximity to water has played a very decisive role in it developing into a major port town for the British and later into India's financial capital. Even though Mumbai today comprises about four hundred and fifty square kilometres[11] in a single land mass, it once used to be an archipelago of seven swampy islands, inhabited mainly by local fishermen called Kolis.

In 1534, the Portuguese seized control of these islands, naming it *Bom Bahia*, meaning the 'Good Bay' in Portuguese, which was later corrupted to 'Bombay' by the British. In 1661 this small collection of islands was handed over to the English. King Charles II received it as part of his dowry when he married the Portuguese Princess Catherine of Braganza. The islands were subsequently leased to the English East India Company in 1668, which recognized the potential of developing Bombay's great harbour. With Bombay growing in importance and population as a trading town, the Company decided to relocate its trading headquarters from Surat to Bombay in 1686. It undertook a number of land reclamation projects that transformed the scattered collection of islands into a bustling mercantile and industrial town from where the Company maintained their trade and authority. In doing so, they established the city's links with the rest of the world and sowed the seeds for what would become India's financial capital.

Bombay's origins as a colonial town also ensured its 'dual city' structure: a city segregated between the colonizers who resided in the organized fortified 'white town' built in 1715 (in the now historic Fort area), and the majority of the local inhabitants who lived in the chaotic, over-crowded and unsanitary settlements north of the Esplanade, in an area commonly referred to as the 'native town'.

Over the next century, Bombay continued to grow, with the Fort as its focal centre, but its growth remained modest until the American Civil War began in 1861, which led to the supply of raw cotton to England being blocked. With the British Lancashire mills now dependent on Bombay for their supply of cotton, the city grew at an amazing pace, and – aided as well by the opening of the Suez Canal in 1869 – its future as the most important port city in India was secured. Moreover, by the time both these events had taken place, Bombay was no longer under the administrative control of the East India Company. The Revolt of 1857 had prompted the British government to assume full control of the city; by then they had come to view Bombay and its fort not only as an essential element in the western defence, but also as a crucial trade link between India and Great Britain.

With the fortified town already very densely built up, and realizing the need to structure growth in the expanding city, the British decided to eliminate the fortifications in the 1860s. This resulted in massive redevelopment and land reclamation that restructured the Fort area at the southern end of the island and reinforced its position as the urban centre of the entire city. This was also the location from where the British built two railway lines that in turn would structure Bombay's growth along a north-south axis.

Being an island where the city's most important functions were located on its narrowest southern stretch of land ensured three things. Firstly, it created an over-dependency on the south, forcing massive flows of traffic towards the business district in the south in the mornings, and in the reverse direction in the evenings. Secondly, it established high real estate prices that would dominate

[10] A REFERENCE TO CHARLES CORREA'S 1976 DOCUMENTARY *A City on the Water*.

[11] BURDETT, R & SUDJIC, D (2011). *Living in the Endless City*. London: Phaidon Press.

how the city and its people were to be compartmentalized (with the affluent residing in the south and the majority of the population in the north). And thirdly, being an island city with only one connection across the harbour meant a constant shortage of land – especially land that could house the city's ever-increasing migrant population. Thus, by the time India gained independence in 1947, it was clear that the city was in dire need of a major restructuring.

[12] **CORREA, C & FRAMPTON, K (1997).** *Charles Correa.* London: Thames & Hudson. 164-165.

MODERNIZATION: THE EXPLODING METROPOLIS

After gaining independence in 1947, India's first Prime Minister Jawarharlal Nehru ushered the country into an era of modernization brought about by increased industrialization and a focus on cities. As the national agenda shifted from agriculture to industry, Bombay continued to witness an ever-increasing number of migrants who came to work in the city's many manufacturing and industrial sites.

By the 1950s, Bombay had transformed tremendously and so had its boundaries. With the establishment of a Greater Bombay region already in place, several studies and recommendations at the time (such as the *Modak-Mayer Plan* of 1947) recognized the need to reorient the city and decongest the overcrowded and heavily burdened southern core. Moreover, by the 1960s Bombay's population had already grown to 4.5 million – and was expected to double to 9 million over the next twenty years.[12] Yet, despite being aware of these alarming statistics, and ignoring earlier recommendations, the Bombay municipality published their *Development Plan* in 1964 that offered no change in strategy to deal with these growing numbers. On the contrary, it proposed even further extensions to the north with the development of a new business district in the northern suburbs of Bandra and Kurla, while at the same time encouraging further densification in the already congested southern core.

Reacting sharply to this plan, two young architects, Charles Correa and Pravina Mehta, and a civil engineer named Shirish Patel, proposed the idea of developing a Twin City across the harbour called 'New Bombay'. Their vision, diametrically opposed to the one proposed by the government, was to convert Bombay's monocentric pattern into a vibrant polycentric one, similar to the model of the Randstad region in the Netherlands or the San Francisco Bay Area in the USA. Their proposal however, hinged on the relocation of the state government headquarters to the new city of New Bombay. This they believed would not only reduce the burden on South Bombay (which housed an enormous number of government buildings), but would also act as a catalyst for growth in the new city.

In the years following 1964, the New Bombay proposal slowly came to be seen as a realistic solution to Bombay's chaotic growth. Finally, in 1970 the Government of Maharashtra accepted its basic principles and set up the *City and Industrial Development Corporation* (CIDCO) to design and develop the new city across the harbour. However, even well into the 1990s only a fraction of the concepts of the New Bombay project had been implemented. The project, which had aimed to solve many of Bombay's growing problems, had not quite lived up to its expectations for three main reasons. Firstly, due to a lack of communication between the CIDCO and the Bombay Municipality. The new city grew in complete isolation from the old, and the planned connections across the harbour were never built. Secondly, even while the new city was being built, the government was simultaneously allowing for urbanization in the Vasai-Virar region in north Bombay, which went against the very idea of New Bombay. Thirdly, and perhaps most importantly, the government, which was supposed to relocate its own offices to New Bombay, never moved out of South Bombay. Thus, the new city was denied the very catalyst that could have spurred its growth.

The failure of the government to understand and implement the very essence of the New Bombay project resulted in further exploitation of the island city, and exposed the myopic attitude of the government towards planning in the city. As Charles Correa states, 'cities do not change because of ideas – but because of political will.'[13] And in New Bombay's case, political will was precisely what was missing.

[13] **CORREA, C (2007).** *New Bombay: Marg as an Urban Catalyst. In: Bombay to Mumbai: Changing Perspectives.* Mumbai: Marg Foundation. 314.

GLOBALIZATION: CONTRASTING TRAJECTORIES OF GROWTH

In the year 1991, on the brink of bankruptcy and in tune with international trends, India entered into a new age with a shift in its economic policy that comprised of economic liberalization, privatization and globalization. By opening up India's previously sealed markets, the country began to see a surge in foreign direct investments that altered the physical landscape of cities like Bombay. Yet, in spite of the state's many efforts to brand growth and prosperity in the country under the tag of 'Incredible India', the reality was that the new economic reforms benefited only a section of India's society – and, in fact, led to a further widening of inequalities in India's urban centres.

In the years following economic liberalization, the city (which by 1997 had been renamed Mumbai) witnessed two important changes. Firstly, the influx of foreign capital, coupled with the information technology (IT) boom of the 1990s completely transformed the city's function from that of an industrial centre to a post-industrial service hub. And secondly, this period saw a sudden surge of migration to the city, which resulted in a dramatic rise in informal settlements, as well as a growth of the informal sector.

Moreover, with real estate becoming the biggest source of income for political parties, there was a sudden desire to free up urban land that could be sold in the open market. This trend was most squarely felt in the redevelopment of the mill lands, the cotton mill area in the heart of the city. Once the very 'engines for growth', by the early 1990s the 600 acres (c. 240 ha) of textile mills had become largely obsolete as a result of competition on the rapidly growing global market. With the land itself yielding more than cotton production, mill owners were eager to sell their property to the private sector, which was only too willing to develop such prime real estate. In the following years, the government formed committees (such as the *Charles Correa Committee* in 1996) which were to assist in drawing up an integrated plan for the redevelopment of the entire mill lands. However, despite the many recommendations, the government chose to amend existing policies, which ensured sky-rocketing profits not only for the mill owners and the private developers – but also for the city government itself. In a way, the redevelopment of the mill lands in Parel set the tone for what was to follow.

Over the years, under the pretext of 'cleansing' Mumbai, or of transforming it into a 'Global City' like Shanghai, vast numbers of the city's urban poor were forcibly removed or relocated to outlying areas (thus denying them proximity to the very jobs they had come for in the first place). Economic liberalization had in fact marked a fundamental shift in the role of the state in matters of housing. Following recommendations proposed by the *World Bank*, the creation of housing supply in India was now left to the private sector, with the state merely acting as a facilitator in the process.

By the turn of the century, more than half of Mumbai's population was living in informal settlements, as the production of affordable housing was unable to keep up with demand. Even the *Slum Rehabilitation Scheme* (a programme introduced in 1995 that enabled developers to rebuild slums on existing plots in exchange for construction rights for buildings they could sell in the open market) failed to improve the living conditions of the urban poor. Instead, a majority of these projects ended up destroying the livelihoods of thousands of slum dwellers whose networks of commerce and employment were broken in the new standardized, inflexible buildings, destined to become 'vertical slums'.

Rendered homeless or unemployed one way or the other, many of the city's urban poor were simply left to accommodate themselves in whatever interstitial spaces they could find. These could be vacant stretches of land near beaches, alongside railway tracks or stretches of mangroves, next to high-end residential towers, malls, or even former industrial sites. In short, a large number of these informal settlements filled in whatever crevices the 'formal' city had not yet 'developed'. As Mehrotra states, this often led to a phenomenon where 'two completely different worlds cohabit the same urban space'[14] – a phenomenon that was going to become even more evident with the introduction of a new typology of dwelling, already popular abroad, called 'gated communities'. Essentially heavily guarded, self-sufficient residential complexes, these communities grew out of the desire to create mini worlds for the rich (complete with shopping malls, fitness centres and movie theatres) that were completely insulated from the growing population of urban poor surrounding them. Sometimes referred to as 'Privatopias',[15] these new walled townships became the symbols of a 'New India' and began to arise both within the city (in the form of vertical gated communities), and on its outskirts (where land was still available).

The emergence of these new typologies of dwelling represented the changed attitude of the state and the rich towards the urban poor. Rather than trying to improve their living conditions and eradicating poverty, the sight of the urban poor in cities like Mumbai was met with strategies that either excluded them from the formal city, or made them 'invisible'. In many ways, the walled towns that had previously been built in the colonial era seem to have resurfaced in recent years to perform the same function.

14 **MEHROTRA, R & DWIVEDI, S (2001).** *Bombay: The Cities Within*. Mumbai: Eminence Designs Pvt. Ltd.

15 **MEHROTRA, R & SHETTY, P (2008).** Frothing Urbanisms. In: Rahul Mehrotra, Pankaj Joshi, Prasad Shetty and Benita Menezes eds. (2008) *Mumbai Reader* Mumbai: UDRI. 13.

MUMBAI: LOOKING AHEAD

In a city of the size and intensity of Mumbai, the scale of problems can often seem overwhelming, and even unmanageable. However, the future is not as bleak as it may seem. Several physical as well as political adjustments, if implemented, could greatly minimize many of the city's drawbacks, and improve the quality of life for all of its citizens. There is an urgent need, perhaps, to look at Mumbai in its larger regional – or even national – context. While there is definitely a need to increase Mumbai's own absorptive capacity, enormous opportunities are to be had in making better use of India's balanced network of cities and its current rapid urbanization to further develop the country's smaller towns and cities. By converting these second and third-tier cities into the country's next growth centres, a lot of the pressure could effectively be diverted from cities like Mumbai and New Delhi.

There are also cues that Mumbai could take from other cities. New York, for example, is only what it should be – a financial capital. It does not carry the burden of being the capital of the state of New York. That responsibility is in the hands of Albany. Similarly, if the state government were to relocate Maharashtra's capital to Navi Mumbai (as was originally planned), large amounts of land in South Mumbai could then be used to meet other critical demands. Moreover, such a shift could lead to the city coming under the much-needed guidance of an elected Mayor who – unlike the Chief Minister today – would be directly responsible for the day-to-day management of the city. Surely a city that contributes close to 40 percent of the nation's taxes deserves such attention.

If such plans were to be actually carried out, it would also be relevant to see Navi Mumbai's role in this new context. Perhaps, along with the planned *Trans Harbour Link*, a 22-kilometre bridge due to be completed by 2017, Navi Mumbai would then finally receive the necessary stimulus to truly become an independent city – and not just remain the far-off suburb it is today. Furthermore, multiple opportunities lie within the island city itself – especially in the recycling of post-industrial wastelands. Ever since the 1980s the city has been moving towards a post-industrial phase, and like other cities across the world (Rotterdam, London, Hamburg) it has rendered several of its manufacturing and industrial sites either redundant or semi-redundant. The Docklands, or eastern waterfront, are a good example. Once the very nucleus of growth, today only about 50 percent of the Dockland's 1800 acres (730 ha) are used for port activities, with other activities having already been relocated or rendered obsolete. By opening up this vital stretch of land (and learning from past mistakes made during the redevelopment of the mill lands), Mumbai and its citizens could benefit from an abundance of public spaces and buildings that could be developed along the 18-kilometre waterfront.

Although Mumbai has a lot to learn from other cities, one must not forget that the city itself has many lessons to offer. The growing informal settlements (which seem to be the city's most crucial problem) are actually wonderful examples of intensive mixed-use development. Dharavi, often referred to as Asia's largest slum, with more than 600,000 residents, is far more than just a place of substandard housing. With industries intrinsically knitted into its residential fabric, it is believed to annually produce goods worth over an astonishing USD 500 million.[16] This makes a settlement like Dharavi not only a vibrant community full of housing, commerce, and employment, but also a substantial contributor to the city's GDP.

In addition, it is important to remind ourselves that, in spite of all of Mumbai's problems, it remains one of the few examples of a city in the developing world whose growth was structured on public transport. Often, in cities around the world, public transport remains an after-thought that follows city growth – making it both difficult to implement, as well as expensive to construct infrastructure for. But, in the case of Mumbai, it actually played a leading role in facilitating growth and opening up urban land. According to recent research by the London School of Economics, close to 35 percent of Mumbai's population uses public transport, and an additional 55 percent walks or cycles to work every day. With a mere 29 cars per 1000 residents, Mumbai boasts of one of the lowest levels of car ownership found in any of the world's major metropolises.

[16] **THE ECONOMIST (2005)** *Inside the Slums.* The Economist. India Edition. 27 January 2005. Available: http://www.economist.com/node/3599622

This in fact makes Mumbai a far more sustainable city than a lot of other First World cities (Los Angeles, for example, has almost 80 percent of its workforce driving to work every day).[17]

Above all else, the history of Mumbai has shown that cities are not only places of work – but places of hope. As Suketu Mehta pointed out: 'For the young person in an Indian village, the call of Mumbai isn't just about money. It's also about freedom.'[18] This is why cities like Mumbai are so crucial for India's future. As we rapidly move closer to Mike Davis's prediction of a city of 33 million people, perhaps the key to Mumbai's success hinges on its ability to achieve a balance between the old and the new, the formal and the informal, and the global and the local. Rather than blindly importing western models of development, we should instead pause to learn and build on the uniqueness and diversity of Mumbai. As Phillip Rode claims, Mumbai is a 'Compact Megacity'[19] – a city with a rich history of intensive mixed use, built and structured on public transport. In that respect, Mumbai has much to teach the world.

17 **BURDETT, R & SUDJIC, D (2011)**. *Living in the Endless City.* London: Phaidon Press. 20.

18 **MEHTA, S (2009)**. Maximum City. In: *Urban Age. Urban India: Understanding the Maximum City.* London: London School of Economics. 43-44. Available: http://v0.urban-age.net/0_downloads/UrbanAgeIndiaNewspaper-web.pdf

19 **RODE, PHILIPP (2009)**. Mumbai: the Compact Mega City. In: *Urban Age: Urban India: Understanding the Maximum City.* London: London School of Economics. 45-46. Available: http://v0.urban-age.net/0_downloads/UrbanAgeIndiaNewspaper-web.pdf

VIEW FROM WORLI FORT

PUBLIC TRANSPORT AS DNA

CHARLES CORREA

Charles Correa (1930) was born in Hyderabad India and studied at the University of Michigan in Ann Arbor and at the Massachusetts Institute of Technology, Cambridge (both in the USA). In 1958 he started his own practice in Mumbai (then Bombay). He is renowned for his adaptations of Modernism to non-Western scenarios, as well as for his emphasis on using local resources and designing structures and town plans in a context-sensitive way.

His portfolio includes new town Navi Mumbai, for which he was Chief Architect from 1970-1975.

He has been awarded with the highest honours, including the Aga Khan Award for Architecture, the Praemium Imperiale of Japan and the Gold Medals of the International Union of Architects (UIA) and the Royal Institute of British Architects (RIBA), the Padma Shri Award and the Padma Vibushan Award from the Government of India.

The most essential characteristic of Bombay, one which distances it from all the other cities of India, is its public transport. This is of crucial benefit to the average citizen. It helps mitigate many of the horrendous things that are happening to the city.

The public transport that characterizes Bombay was not an afterthought. It was an essential element in the DNA of the city – right from the 1870s, when Bombay's growth started to really accelerate. The Suez Canal had just been opened and the American Civil War had cut off the supply of cotton to the mills of Lancashire. These two crucial events enabled the British to implement their earlier decision to make this city their gateway into India. So through extensive land fill, they connected the seven islands to form an elongated landmass that is really an extended breakwater, protecting the harbour from the open sea. The port is located at the southern end of this breakwater, and from this point the British constructed two major railway systems, which became the life-blood of India, carrying goods and passengers across the country. One of them, the Great Indian Peninsular Railway (GIP) ran the 'Calcutta Mail' to take businessmen to Calcutta; the other, the Bombay, Baroda and Central Indian Railway (BB&CI) ran the 'Frontier Mail' carrying troops up to the Khyber Pass.

Starting at the southern end of the city, both lines travel roughly parallel to each other, up the length of Bombay island. Crossing Mahim Creek, they part ways: the BB&CI continues northward to Karachi, while the GIP swerves in a north-easterly direction towards Calcutta. The railway authorities constructed stations along these two routes, and people began to live around these stations —thus sowing the seeds of Bombay's extended suburbs.

It was as direct as that. The urban structure of Bombay was not ordained by any city planner, but really was determined by the railway engineers who created those two arteries. It is a structure that has played a decisive role in the phenomenal success of the city. Around these railway stations, the city grew – housing people who needed affordable transport to get to their work in the mills of Parel, or in the offices of south Bombay. This corridor of demand created by Bombay's linear structure makes possible a much higher frequency of trains than in the evenly distributed sprawl of Chennai, Delhi or Calcutta— and this in turn makes the fares lower and the service more attractive. In short: in the case of Bombay, supply preceded demand—and in the process generated the structure of the city. Stations of interchange between the two railway lines, like Dadar or Bandra, of course grew more swiftly – because they provided even greater access to economic opportunity. It is precisely this mobility, this interaction, available to all its citizens, that is the essence of Bombay's success. (Perhaps the real goal of city planners should not be the City Beautiful, but really the City as Network, as Synergy?)

II

Migrants don't come to cities looking for housing. They come in search of work. And they try to live as close as possible to their workplaces – or to some form of transport that will take them to those places. Thus affordable urban housing is not an isolated problem – it is the product of an equation that includes at least two other crucial parameters: job location and available transport. In India, very few people have access to cars—this is why public transport (trains, buses and trams) is of such crucial importance to them. It means they can get to their job, their school, their doctor, their friends. Much is made of the energy, the get-up-and-go spirit of Bombay – especially as compared to Calcutta and Delhi. But do we ever ask ourselves: how much of this is due to the greater mobility of the average citizen? After all, cities are about interaction – and the synergy that it generates.

A mass transport system is, by definition, linear. To provide economical service, it needs to operate within a corridor of high-density demand. An even sprawl of low-density demand cannot sustain an economical public transport system. Today our cities are either laid out as a matrix of sectors, as for instance Chandigarh, or they are allowed to grow haphazardly, unstructured by any transport systems. Then, decades later, when we attempt to inlay a system of Mass Rapid Transport (MRT), we find it exorbitantly expensive to build. Furthermore, its operation has to be heavily subsidized, because of the lack of any corridors of high-density demand. Delhi's new Metro is a case in point. Subsidized at great expense by the central government for the national capital, it is not a solution that India's other metropoli will find easy to replicate.

So trying to retrofit public transport systems after the city has developed is a very expensive proposition. But what if – as happened in the case of Bombay – we integrate public transport with land-use, right from the start. It will be cheaper to build – and will also structure the city along high-density corridors, making the system more efficient to operate. In Bombay, a train ticket, valid for an unlimited number of journeys for a whole month, from Andheri to the city centre (a distance of about thirty km), costs less than three euros per month – which is a very affordable price. And even if this involves some subsidy on the transport system, it is really an indirect subsidy on housing, since the MRT opens up more urban land, thus bringing the price of housing down to affordable levels.

The same trade-off operates in North America – except there the suburbs are being cross-subsidized by colossal highway construction programmes. This is a trade-off that many Americans consider disastrous, since private cars commuting along these freeways and express roads have helped destroy cities right across the US. Unfortunately, this is not understood by India's urban elite. In our rush to imitate the lifestyles of the West, automobiles are proliferating in our cities – leading to ever bigger traffic jams. And so the next step is already well underway: the demand for more and bigger expressways and flyovers, connecting inner cities to outer suburbs and so forth – all of which comes with a huge price tag that we can ill afford. It is a tragedy of truly epic proportions.

Which brings us to the final clincher, which is this: Bombay's railways were not built to squander wealth – but to generate it. The GIP and the BB&CI, as well as the other railways of India, were all funded by private capital – as were the railways of Europe and North America. And the investors made a lot of money doing this. Vanderbilt, Morgan, Harriman – the great fortunes of the robber barons of the 19th century were generated by the railroads they invested in. It is a crucial fact that we must understand if we are going to address our urban problems within the context of our economic constraints. Especially so if we ever try to really comprehend the humongous scale of growth that lies ahead – according to our own predictions!

III

The scale of urban growth that lies ahead – that's the key issue. It makes the problems of our cities fundamentally different from those in the West. The populations of most European and North American nations are either declining, or stagnant – with an urban percentile that is already higher than eighty percent. So their cities are not really growing – at most, some marginal adjustments might occur here and there, as a small percent of the population moves from one city to another. This is why most of the urban strategies developed by the academics and professionals in the West are principally concerned with 'fine-tuning'.

But the urban crisis erupting all over the developing world calls for far more dynamic responses – and on quite another scale. Consider the growth of the squatter colonies in Bombay. Starting in the late 1950s, by 1964 they were ten percent of the population of 4.5 million. In that year, the government published their development plan which estimated a population of eight million by 1985. But by 1985, the squatters had grown from ten percent to fifty percent, i.e., four million people! Today the city's population is sixteen million – of which the government estimates the squatters to constitute sixty percent, i.e., almost ten million people!

This is why the lessons of Bombay's original DNA are of such crucial importance. Because of the two railway corridors we have been discussing, the city had no squatter colonies right up to World War II – despite the waves of migrants that were pouring in. Squatter colonies started to appear only in the 1950s – an explicit signal that public transport was not opening up new land fast enough, and so demand had started to overwhelm supply. We should have responded by creating new job centres in new locations, connected by new MRTs. This is what Navi Mumbai was all about – a restructuring of Bombay's growth toward the hinterland of the state, through the development of new growth centres and new lines of public transport. (But unfortunately, those strategies were never implemented by the State Government—or perhaps even understood.)

ENVOI

Of all the colossal metropolises of our contemporary world, London is, in my experience, the most livable. Why? Because it not only has parks and terrace houses with gardens, etc., but it also has public transport – buses and trains that take you right across the city. And how did this happen? Because in the early 20th century, the lines of London's Underground were extended beyond the closer suburbs (Hampstead, etc.) to the areas beyond, thus opening up a great deal of new territory. Later, in the 1920s the developers followed, creating housing communities. In short: London's public transport is a wonderful example of how public transport can structure a city's growth – supply generating demand, with very successful results. And this reiterates the invaluable lesson that Bombay's DNA should have already taught us: viz., that public transport cannot be the last to enter the scene – in fact, given the scale of growth that lies ahead, there are crucial advantages in making sure it is one of the first.

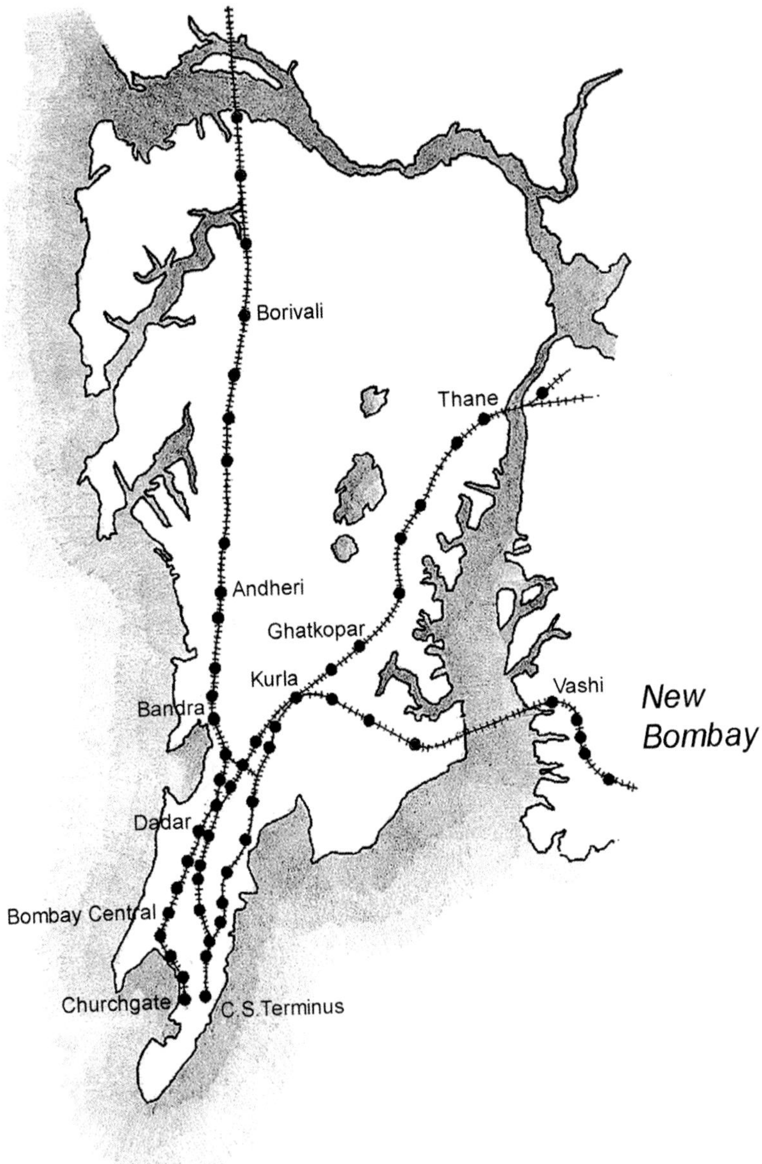

DEMAND FOLLOWS SUPPLY: THE RAILWAY ARTERIES THAT CREATED BOMBAY

VIEW FROM GOVANDI RAILWAY STATION

VIEW FROM CHARNI ROAD RAILWAY STATION, GIRGAON

REMAKING MUMBAI

RAHUL MEHROTRA

Rahul Mehrotra (1959) studied at the School of Architecture, Ahmedabad and at the Graduate School of Design at Harvard University. He started his own firm in 1990, *Rahul Mehrotra Associates*, which currently has offices in Mumbai and Boston, MA (USA).

He is actively involved in urban conservation projects in Mumbai and has served from 1992 to 1999 on the Advisory Committee to the Municipal Commissioner on the conservation of heritage buildings and artifacts in the city of Mumbai.

He is also the Executive Director of the Urban Design Research Institute, which promotes awareness and research on the city of Mumbai. He has written several books on Mumbai and has lectured extensively on urban design, conservation and architecture, with a special focus on developments in India. At present he is an associate professor at the University of Michigan, Anne Arbor (USA).

By exploring the urban potential of some of Mumbai's most sensitive sites, such as the mill lands and its eastern waterfront, Rahul Mehrotra challenges the design professions and civic leaders not to squander the opportunity of 'remaking' Mumbai for the better.

Over the last three decades in Mumbai, planning has been largely concerned with rearguard actions versus the avant-garde approaches that traditionally led planning. Thus today most infrastructure follows city growth rather than facilitating and opening up new growth centres within and outside the city's core. In contemporary Mumbai, planning happens systematically 'posterior', as a recuperative and securing action.[1] Perhaps globalization and the urgency of integrating with a broader economic system are challenging the priorities of the governing authorities responsible for making the city? The case of the mill lands vividly illustrates the city's runaway physical growth. In the development of the area's 2.37 km^2, located in the crowded central district of Parel, the economic gain of a select few has driven the conversion of this rare asset into private commercial development. Yet, despite being a vitally important and heavily publicised planning decision, no planning agency in Mumbai prepared a masterplan or strategy to integrate these lands for the benefit of the city; and concerned citizens, environmentalists and planners just reacted too late to salvage whatever could be retrieved through Public Interest Litigation (PIL) within a set of legislative moves to divide this prime land.

In sum, the mill lands demonstrate the state of the profession of urban planning and the culture of architecture in the city. Here, professionals and institutions are seemingly unequipped to grapple with emergent issues in the city. Thus, the profession is chiefly engaged in recuperative action, intervening post-facto to clean up the mess! It is therefore no coincidence that in Mumbai there is an increased celebration of projects involving 'cleaning up' – whether that is the restoration of historic buildings, precincts or districts, waterfronts and pavements, or the relocation of slums to make way for infrastructure. While critical to the functioning of the city, these projects are an indication of the limited role of the architectural and engineering professions as well as all the other agencies involved in making the city. By default, the private sector is determining the emergent form of Mumbai. This is the result of a fundamental shift in the planning process whereby the government has privatised city development. And although the government has devolved itself of the responsibility of delivering urban amenities within a strategic framework, it has not defined its new role. Will it still be the custodian of the public realm or will it establish the checks and balances required for the unleashing of private enterprise for urban development?

Today, there is an incredible disjuncture in the city between existing and allocated land use and the positioning of new infrastructure – a condition where land use, transportation planning and urban form have no relationships with each other in the emergent landscape.[2] How then do growth, planning and vision for the city accommodate the future?

In order to evolve an approach relevant to this emerging scenario, there needs to be greater engagement with city issues by the citizens and professionals in the city. To allow this to happen, planning or decisionmaking about urban form

1 LIM, WSW (2005). *Asian Ethical Urbanism – A Radical Post-modern Perspective*, Introduction by Van Schaik, Leon, Singapore, 31–32.

2 Developed in studies carried out through the UDRI Mumbai Studio by Pankaj Joshi and participants in the Fellowship Program.

should be addressed at two levels – the macro (or city) level and the micro or area/ neighbourhood level. In this model, akin to the state and concurrent lists at the national policy level, the macro level would concern itself with infrastructure, roads and connections between parts of the city as well as broad policies for the metropolitan area. At the micro level, issues of urban form – FSI (floor space index) and TDR (transfer of development right) designations, aesthetics as well as health and hygiene – would enable city authorities to take responsibility for orchestrating growth in the region with the local level organisations (i.e. ward offices or citizens' groups) focused on the tactics for urban governance. This decentralised system would be far more efficient in managing as well as responding to crisis situations – like smaller pixels on a screen, we will get higher resolution in our cities on the ground.

Cities grow and evolve by opening up new land for growth or recycling land within their domains. In both these processes, people affected must necessarily participate in the process if the decisions are to be sustainable. The misappropriation of the mill lands demonstrates that without this engagement, land becomes an abstract entity reduced to blobs of colour on a land use plan – open to change and manipulation. Cities by nature are contested territories. Who commands what and how in a democracy is determined by who participates or is excluded from the process. It is crucial that a city has an articulated strategy for its growth and builds a consensus reflecting the aspiration of its citizens. In the mill lands, the state government and planning agencies sadly did not engage its citizens in the process of adapting this asset for future growth.

In this context, the eastern waterfront is of great relevance to the city and the region, as the connection between the latter two depends on how the eastern water's edge is recycled for use. In the regional growth scenarios and projections of the Golden Triangle (connecting Mumbai, Nashik and Pune), the eastern waterfront could connect the old centre with the regional triangle's emergent industries, special economic and agricultural export zones. This land also offers the potential to connect the peripheral areas of the city with the Metropolitan region as a whole.

The eastern waterfront's approximately 7.3 km^2 (1,800 acres / 730 ha) are grappling with great transformation as the economy of Mumbai moves into the post-industrial phase. While this area is roughly 3 times larger than the area of the mill lands, interestingly only 6 percent of this land is under reservation by the BMC for public use, which is a meagre 0.85 percent of open space. Thus the area's stretch of 14.5 km of virtually inaccessible waterfront offers the potential for public access while reorienting the perception of the region with regard to the city's geography and physical form. Similarly, the potential for connectivity using water transport could offer the much-needed transformation of mobility within the region.

Currently only 50 percent of the land, 3.4 km^2 (836 acres / 340 ha), is used for port activities. Large, seemingly underused infrastructure, roads and warehouses (often beautifully robust buildings with great reuse potential) create a sense of desolation that is offset by teeming populations, labour pools and a virtual sea of energy and resources creating new forms of employment in the area. Equally daunting is determining the process most appropriate to trigger the conversion of this incredible resource of land, people and infrastructure to improve the city while safeguarding the interest of present users? Indeed, the ecology of the region, defined by the mangroves and flamingos that settle here during half the year, couple with the heritage buildings and treasures such as the Sewri Fort and other fragments to comprise the rich fabric of Mumbai's eastern waterfront.[3] The eastern waterfront is a crucial zone that could transform Mumbai and compensate for the city's many physical deficiencies. The challenge is how to rearrange the landscape to synergize these different components.

This essay is adapted from a longer analysis of the planning situation in Mumbai entitled 'Post Planning in Mumbai'. The essay appeared in the book Mills for Sale: the Way Ahead, *published by MARG publications, Mumbai, December 2006.*

[3] *A Study of the eastern waterfront of Mumbai.* A situation analysis carried out between August 2000 and December 2001 and published by the Urban Design Research Institute in Mumbai in 2005. This document contains a detailed mapping of the eastern waterfront and the potential for its recycling.

VIEW OF EASTERN WATERFRONT AREA, WADI BANDAR

AP
TRANSPORT

FACTS AND FIGURES

TIMO CENTS

Timo Cents (1982) studied Landscape Architecture at the Larenstein University of Applied Sciences in Arnhem (the Netherlands) and at the Technical University of Berlin. He continued his studies at the Utrecht University (the Netherlands). Research for his Master's thesis in Urban Planning brought him to Mumbai in 2009. It was conducted under the umbrella of a larger project, called *Respace*, which was led by Bart Wissink (City University of Hong Kong). This project focused on enclave urbanism in five Asian city regions: Bangkok, Guangzhou, Hong Kong, Tokyo, and Mumbai. Timo's extensive fieldwork in the city culminated in a thesis entitled: *The Manufacturing of Informality. Informal Settlements in Mumbai in an Actor-Network Perspective*. He currently works at *ARCADIS Landscape-Architecture* and is involved in a broad range of projects throughout the Netherlands.

For his master thesis Timo Cents spent several months collecting data in Mumbai on informal settlements, or slums, as they are more commonly known. He struggled to find reliable facts and figures about the city. 'Putting two research papers or reports together would give me two different sets of data, putting three papers together would give me three date sets', he recalls. 'To retrieve the most up-to-date information we visited a government body whose aim it is to make Mumbai slum-free by 2020. We figured that if they wanted to embark on that task, they would at least have an overview of Mumbai's informal settlements: how many people inhabit them, where they are exactly located, what kind of facilities they have... etcetera.'

'We asked a government official sitting in a room on the ground floor if his department indeed had the task to make Mumbai slum-free. He confimed this. And when we said we assumed that he then must have done quite some data collection to get a good idea of the extent of informal housing in the city, he granted this again. But when we asked "Can you share your data with us?" the official was less certain all of a sudden, and said: "Oh, what you want is not with us, you have to go to the office located one floor *above* this one and ask the staff there". We did as we were told, but you can imagine that by the time we reached the eleventh floor of the building, we were quite frustrated. It hit us that even *if* they had the information, they would probably not share it with us.'

Yet, Timo found it is not *impossible* to get good data. 'The *Centre for Documentation and Education* in Colaba turned out to be a valuable alternative source of information. We found a wealth of material there in the form of newspaper clippings.' Another good source were NGOs like the *Society for the Promotion of Area Resource Centres* (SPARC). 'For some infrastructure projects, *SPARC* was assigned a role as the official mediator between the slum-dwellers and the government; a precarious role, but it does give them, where it exists, access to detailed government data of the settlements', he explains.

TABLES, GRAPHS AND MAPS

Timo made his own maps to present the data he collected for his study. A few of these are reproduced in this volume to illustrate some of the major trends in the urban development of Mumbai. The table and graph on page 42 highlight the excessive population density of Mumbai, and the exponential growth of its formal and informal population. The map on page 43 presents the land use in Mumbai. 'As you can see, not only *informal* settlements are built on protected land, such as inside the *Sanjay Gandhi National Park*, and sensitive areas like the mangroves', Timo points out. 'In the heated debates over land use in the city this is easily forgotten, but in reality encroaching is done by slum-dwellers and formal builders alike.' The map on page 44 shows the land reclamation and the relation between industry, transport, and housing. Finally, the six maps on page 45 show the process of urbanization over time. 'What is really remarkable is the level of integration of the slums within the city', Timo says. 'This is not a model where those who can't find formal housing are pushed out. It is more complex than that: even in very upmarket areas you find informal settlements.'

POPULATION DENSITIES ACROSS THE WORLD

City	Population	Area (km^2)	People per Hectare
Mumbai	13,922,125	603	23,088
Mexico City	8,836,045	1,485	5,950
Beijing	10,123,000	1,368	7,400
London	7,683,316	1,580	4,863
Amsterdam	752,911	219	4,457

Source: World Gazetteer, 2009.

POPULATION DEVELOPMENT IN MUMBAI

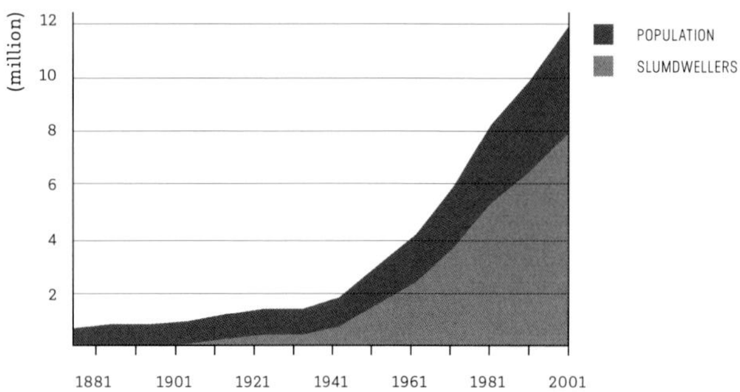

Cents, Timo. 2009. *The Manufacturing of Informality. Informal Settlements in Mumbai.*

URBAN CHARACTERISTICS OF MUMBAI, DELHI AND AHMEDABAD

City	Income (INR*/cap)	Area (sq.km)	Vehicle Population (million)		Vehicle Density (vehicles/1,000 people)	
			1991	2005	1991	2005
Mumbai	400,000	603	0.63	1.29	50	69
Delhi	449,190	1,483	1.81	4.19	216	279
Ahmedabad	188,640	1,300	0.37	1.63	112	321

*1 INR = 0.0128 EUR = 0.0168 USD (July 2013). Source: Census Bureau, NCEAR data, 2006.

POWER CONSUMPTION IN MUMBAI

	2006	2012	2015
Daily power consumption (MW)	2,555	3,288	4,174
Generation capacity (MW)		2,277	
Imported capacity (MW)		950	

Source: Times of India. 2011. *Thirst for Power Will See Demand in Mumbai Rise by 886MW.* 27 October.

LAND USE IN MUMBAI

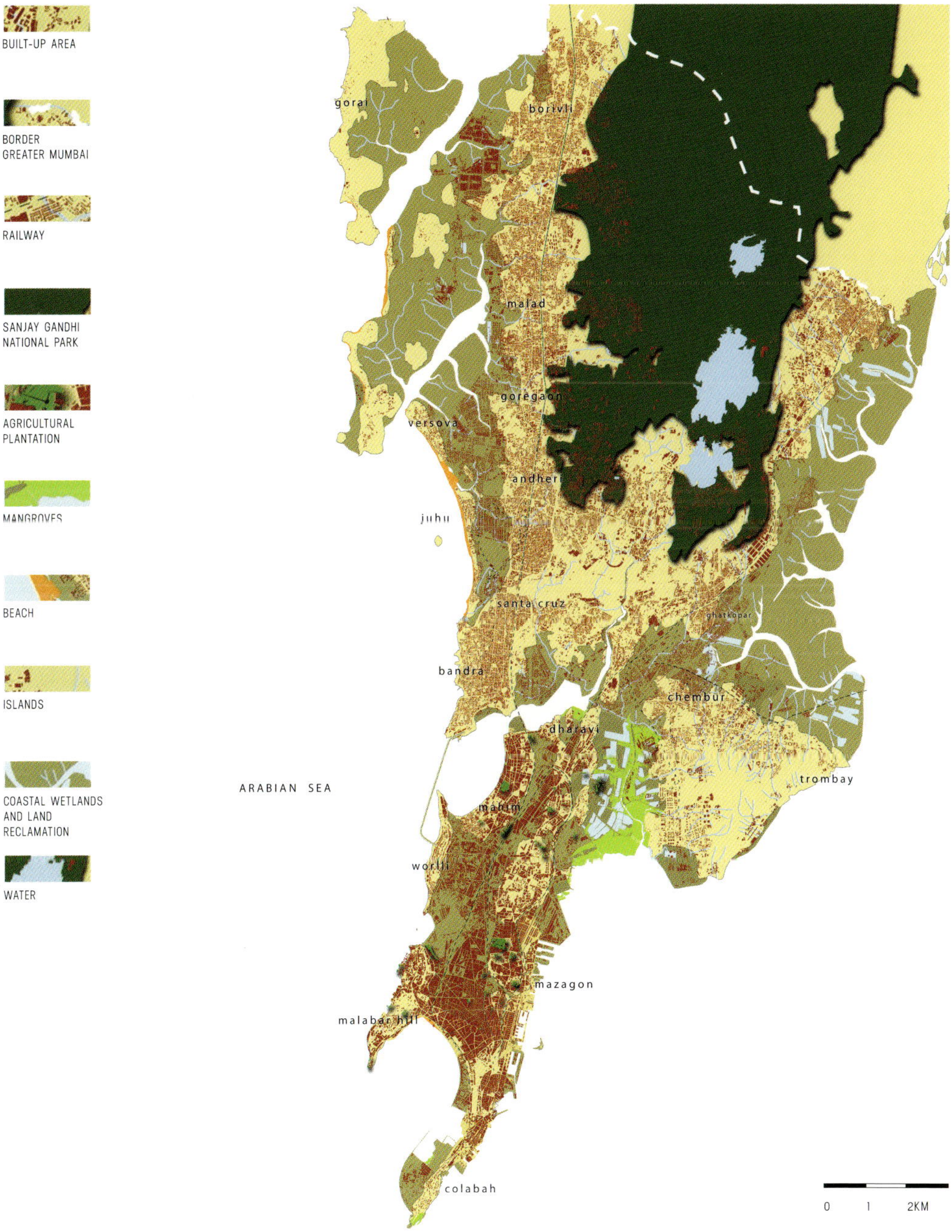

Cents, Timo. 2009. *The Manufacturing of Informality. Informal Settlements in Mumbai.*

MUMBAI 1869-1964

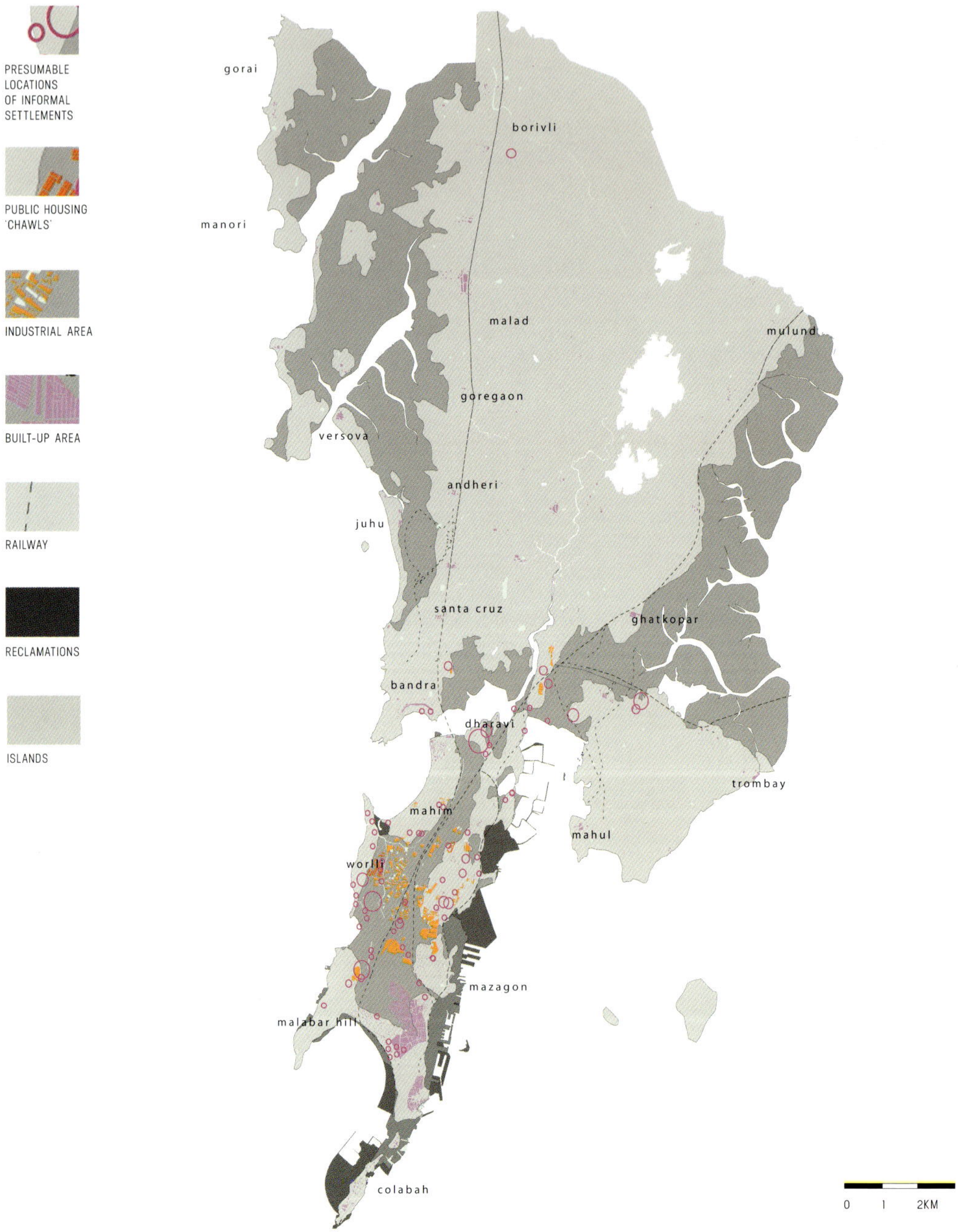

Cents, Timo. 2009. *The Manufacturing of Informality. Informal Settlements in Mumbai.*

URBANISATION OF MUMBAI OVER TIME (INCLUDING INFORMAL SETTLEMENTS)

Cents, Timo. 2009. *The Manufacturing of Informality. Informal Settlements in Mumbai.*

INTERVIEWS

INTERVIEWS
INTERVIEWS
INTERVIEWS
INTERVIEWS
INTERVIEWS
INTERVIEWS
INTERVIEWS
INTERVIEWS
INTERVIEWS
INTERVIEWS
INTERVIEWS
INTERVIEWS

APPRECIATING THE UNCONTROLLED AND THE UNEXPECTED

STEVEN BEUNDER

Steven Beunder (1969) studied Urban Design at TU Delft in the Netherlands, Urban Planning at Middlesex University in London, UK and Human Geography and Urban Planning at Utrecht University in the Netherlands.

In 2004 he joined *Townland Consultants* as principal town planner. He worked on master planning projects in various Asian countries. In 2008 Steven moved to Mumbai. After a brief period with *Aedas Urban Design & Landscape* in Mumbai, as head of Urban Design India, he rejoined *Townland Consultants* as an associate master planner in 2009.

He now manages the Indian office and leads a team of urban designers on a wide variety of urban design, master planning and conceptual architecture projects throughout India. At present *Townland Consultants* is working (together with *Edifice Consultants*) on one of the biggest planning projects in the city: a master plan for a new business district in Wadala.

After ten years of working for several urban design firms in the Netherlands, Indonesia and Hong Kong, in 2008 Steven Beunder moved to Mumbai to run the Indian office of Hong Kong based planning and design firm *Townland Consultants*.

'*Townland Consultants* is an international, multi-disciplinary planning and design consultancy providing services to governments, private sector, and development agencies throughout the Asian Pacific region and Africa', Steven explains. 'We offer a host of planning and design services, including urban and regional planning, development consultancy, master planning, urban design, concept architecture and landscape design. The company was founded in Hong Kong in 1985 and has regional offices in Jakarta, Shenzhen, Chengdu and Mumbai. We have delivered over 3,000 projects since establishment and we are considered one of the leading planning and design consultancies in Southeast Asia.'

PLANNING FOR MUMBAI

Over the years, Steven found that successful designing for the Indian market requires achieving a fine balance between planning concepts from the West and ideas and cultural preferences found in India. 'Planning concepts that we are all familiar with in the West, like the value of the human scale, walkability on a neighbourhood level, pedestrian oriented public spaces, and transit oriented development, form a common thread through all our master plans. The concepts and ideas that we can bring to the table are in most cases greatly appreciated by our clients. Yet, we always keep in mind that particular conceptions and beliefs that are important in Indian society may make it difficult to get certain planning concepts that are valued in the West accepted by the client.'

He illustrates this with an example. 'The popularity of the mystical doctrine of *Vastu Shastra* prescribes, among other things, a specific orientation of buildings. Changing this, or, for instance, suggesting vertical mixing of commercial and residential typologies and different building typologies in one neighbourhood, often leads to heated debates, as clients are unfamiliar with it. I found that you get room for experiments and new concepts, as long as your plans do not jeopardize the marketability of the residential units.'

PITFALLS & OPPORTUNITIES FOR FOREIGN FIRMS

Townland is one of only a handful of *foreign* urban design consultants that have set up office in Mumbai. Why are there so few other firms? Steven explains: 'Most foreign architects and urban design firms that work on projects in India are part of large consultancy companies that may have been active in the Asian market for a long time. But since working in India and establishing a firm here is not easy, they decide to keep working from nearby regional offices in Asia, like in Dubai, Singapore or Hong Kong.' The most difficult part is the radically different work environment international firms have to deal with, Steven thinks. 'The project development process of large-scale projects in India, from inception to implementation, is very complex and tends to move slowly. There is a high rate of aborted projects. The reason lies in the constantly changing planning regulations and the unpredictability of a market that is still in its nascent stage.' He emphasizes that Western firms that do not have a permanent presence in South Asia and that have little or no knowledge of how the development process works have limited added value for Indian clients. 'A strong commitment to invest in India for the long run is what Indian developers and government institutes want from their international consultants.'

He does emphasize that there are positive sides as well, and that opportunities exist for urban planners in India. 'It is still relatively easy to distinguish yourself as an international master planner, since urban design is still a new concept among developers. Only in the last five to ten years have Indian developers started to move away from the relatively small suburban "gated communities" towards developing large-scale townships and satellite cities. There is space in the market, because as of now there are only a handful of Indian design firms that offer proper urban design capabilities on par with international standards.'

FOREIGN VERSUS LOCAL IN ARCHITECTURE

When it comes to architecture it is a different story. 'The competition among architects is much more intense', Steven says. 'For the market segment of more prestigious residential and commercial projects, and for projects that require exceptional technical capabilities, international architecture firms are certainly sought after. You see this happening for example with the ultra-luxurious skyscrapers coming up in Mumbai and with the many airports that are being built across the country. But for the majority of the more regular architecture projects, Indian clients generally prefer to work with Indian architects, or with foreign companies firmly based in India. Clients feel that these Indian firms are better able to understand all the intricacies of designing according to local Indian design rules and cultural preferences, like the *Vastu* rules I mentioned before.'

But he sees a more practical reason as well: 'An architect in India often also shoulders the thorny process of helping the client to receive all planning permissions from a string of government bodies on local, state, and sometimes national level. The rules and regulations tend to be complex and often very ambiguous. This part of the design process therefore means the developer prefers to hire a local architect, in particular one who has established the right contacts within the government to keep the development projects moving.'

COMMUNICATION & NETWORKING

One of the important lessons Steven learned over the years is that 'innovative Dutch designers who want to enter the Indian market cannot just rely on the outstanding quality of their work and an impressive portfolio'. 'They have to invest in other skills that are crucial to doing business in India: communication and networking.'

He gives an example from his own experience. 'If I show a potential new client some of our best projects that we've completed in China, even if the scope of work is almost completely similar to their own project, they may not be too impressed. What they basically want to see is your experience of working on similar projects in India, preferably for a client they know personally.' Emphasizing how important these non-technical capacities are, Steven adds, 'Let me put it this way: in my experience, if one could say that in the Netherlands the success of an urban designer depends for 50 percent on his qualities as a designer, and for 50 percent on his qualities as a networker and communicator, in India this would be 20 percent and 80 percent respectively. Having the right network and being able to get your local projects executed is key.'

PATIENCE & FLEXIBILITY

In addition to communication and networking skills there are two more characteristics that architects and planners should possess if they wish to increase their chances for success in India. 'Those who want to take the step and start an office in Mumbai need patience and flexibility as well', Steven advises. 'Patience is required because the process of creating a network of potential clients and landing actual projects takes a while.'

'Each and every project takes longer than anticipated and allocated for', Steven warns. 'On paper the fees are similar to what is paid internationally. But in reality the margins in master planning are lower because of these delays. So you end up doing more work for the same money. That is if you get the money at all! Take it as a rule that the payment always comes late. And don't be surprised if you don't get your full fee. It is not uncommon that the last invoice is not paid at all. It is normal practice now to sign a detailed contract at the start of a project and to get a down payment, but still you have to have a flexible attitude when it comes to the extra design changes and new deliverables a client expects along the way. All in all, the relationship with clients may be quite different than what you are used to in Europe.'

If you are able to work with patience and flexibility, he feels it is worth starting a business in India. 'It is definitely possible to make a decent profit', he says, 'but that is only possible by setting up an office in India itself and by keeping the overhead costs low, with a limited number of expats and a team of internationally educated Indian designers.'

LEARNING FROM...

Mumbai's track record in city planning makes Steven doubtful about what, at present, Dutch urban planners can learn from the city: too few master plans have been realized. 'The most forward thinking visions and large-scale master plans that could potentially make a real impact on the liveability of the city have remained on the drawing board. They stranded on political and bureaucratic obstacles', Steven says. 'However, things seem to be changing slowly. Some of the more ambiguous development control regulations in Mumbai were changed last year. This could potentially have an impact on the way the city is planned. We are noticing the first signs of change already at our office. *Townland* has recently landed two master planning projects for the redevelopment of large former industrial sites that were on hold for three years. Now these will finally kick off.'

Although bureaucracy and politics often tend to have a paralyzing effect on implementing master plans in Indian cities in general, Steven thinks that for Mumbai there is another major crippling factor. 'Since this city lies for a large part on a peninsula, there is such a space crunch in Mumbai that even the implementation of narrow infrastructure corridors for a network of new roads, rail, and metro lines has been very complicated and painfully slow. Other major cities in India, like Delhi, Kolkata, Hyderabad and Bangalore, have in that respect been more successful. In addition to creating several New Towns, these cities have been more expeditious in developing new traffic and public transport infrastructure.' Dutch planners who want to learn more about the current state of affairs in Indian urban planning should study these cities rather than Mumbai, he seems to imply.

MUMBAI AS A KINETIC CITY

That does not mean that Mumbai is not interesting for urban planners to live in or to visit. 'In Mumbai', Steven argues, 'you can learn a lot from, what is, in essence, the opposite of planning: urban development phenomena like the "organic city" or "kinetic city", a term coined by one of the city's most well-known architects, Rahul Mehrotra. You can experience that everywhere.'

'Mumbai is an organic and kinetic city due to the constantly changing scenery one experiences in the public realm', Steven clarifies. 'Mumbai is a city that constantly reinvents itself. The impact of the numerous religious festivals organized by neighbourhood committees, the outdoor wedding parties, the constant stream of new pavement dwellers and hawkers, and the seasonal monsoon rains all together create this kaleidoscope of temporary canopies, tents and structures that appear and disappear on rooftops, in parks, squares and on pavements. And all of this happens in one constant motion, not in a planned manner, but organically and initiated by ordinary citizens.' 'An organic or kinetic city is about letting go', he adds. 'It is about appreciating the qualities of a city in organized chaos and constant flux; about appreciating the uncontrolled and the unexpected. And it is exactly this that makes the city so interesting and alive.'

THE ORGANIC CITY

Steven feels that the way Mumbai grows provides another good example of Mumbai as a kinetic or organic city. 'Look for example at the unplanned transformations taking place in the industrial compounds in the former mill areas of Worli and Parel. Or take the way informal settlements and slums have become an integral part of the urban fabric. For Dutch planners it is interesting to see how even at present cities still can grow organically. To see what happens in a scenario where there is no overarching planning. That, I think, is very similar to the way European cities used to grow and develop until the Renaissance. The result is a surprisingly vibrant city, full of exciting contrasts, a city that never bores.'

Steven gives the example of what he experienced when visiting some of the slums the city. 'Some of the older slums are beautifully situated on the waterfront, like the one in Worli or the one on the hillside of Mount Mary in Bandra. When you walk through these slums it almost makes you feel as if you are transported to a picturesque Mediterranean village: look at the human scale of the built fabric, the balanced variety in built forms, intimate communal areas and the mixture of work, live and play in a tightknit community.' Seeing this organic growth in Mumbai made Steven realize that concepts from New Urbanism need not always be prescribed as urban planning rules. 'Let people free and amazingly these exact rules are what people will naturally follow', he argues. 'The rules are not alien to us; we only seem to have lost this knowledge along the way.' And Mumbai, Steven has found, is a particularly good place to reconnect with it.

'For me personally, but also as an urban planner, these examples of organized chaos in Mumbai's streets and neighbourhoods make it such an inspiring place to live. And even more so when I visit New Town developments in the Netherlands now. There everything is so regulated and designed up to the tiniest details that I cannot escape the notion that they are very well thought through, but for that same reason sometimes also come across as a bit sterile.'

'I guess what my Indian experience has taught me', Steven concludes, 'is that it wouldn't hurt if the planning rules in Dutch cities would be a bit more relaxed, so there is more room for private-citizen and grass-root initiatives.'

MASTER PLAN KASARA HILL TOP TOWNSHIP, THANE, MAHARASHTRA

MASTER PLAN DHARAPUR TOWNSHIP, GUWAHATI, ASSAM

MASTER PLAN NAV SURAT NEW TOWN, SURAT, GUJARAT

ANTILIA, THE 27-FLOOR HOUSE BELONGING TO BUSINESSMAN MUKESH AMBANI

MY MUMBAI
STEVEN BEUNDER

MUMBAI IS SPECIAL BECAUSE
Its people. Not just the friendly, open nature of the people in general, but it also amazes me that, while 50 percent of its citizens live in slums and 20 percent live below the poverty line, Mumbai is one of the safest cities in the world.

THIS CAN BE IMPROVED
Public transportation. Mumbai's trains are notoriously overcrowded. Every day 10 people die by falling of the train or being run over on the tracks! Millions of lives of ordinary Mumbaikars would improve greatly with a proper metro system.

MY FAVOURITE PLACE
My own rooftop terrace.

MY FAVOURITE RESTAURANT
Olive Bar & Kitchen in Bandra. It is a popular Mediterranean restaurant within walking distance from home. They have good food and a great outdoor patio. Al fresco dining all year round: it's one of the great things of Mumbai.

MY FAVOURITE LANDMARK
Antilia. It's the most talked about home in Mumbai. A 27-STORY tower built two years back as a private residence for the richest man in the country: Mukesh Ambani, the chairman of *Reliance Industries*. The building costs are an estimated one billion US dollars! Apparently on the inside it's all gold, marble statues and chandeliers, but at least on the outside it's been quite successful in creating an interesting and current architectural statement.

THE BEST PLACE TO RELAX
The *Breach Candy Club*. It's one of the few clubs in Mumbai where expats can become a short-term member and the club has a great old-world charm to it, with a massive pool, right on the seafront. These members-only clubs are sort of a relic from the colonial days, but still play an important part in the social life of the urban elite. It's a great place to escape to on the weekends, when you want to take a breather from the madness on the streets.

IF ONE THING COULD BE DEMOLISHED IT WOULD BE
The slum rehabilitation blocks on Tulsi Pipe Road in Lower Parel. The density of this complex is mind-boggling. All the 15-story high buildings are set apart no more than three metres. Instead of providing a better lifestyle for the former slum residents, they've created what can only be called a vertical slum.

MY CHOICE OF TRANSPORTATION
Auto rickshaw and bicycle. I am lucky enough to be living and working in the same neighbourhood – Bandra – so it means I don't really need a car.

IF NOT MUMBAI THEN
Definitely Mumbai. I don't think I would ever consider moving to another city in India. It is the colonial past and the multicultural nature of the city that make it the most cosmopolitan and vibrant of the Indian cities, a true metropolis in many ways.

WHAT WE CAN LEARN FROM MUMBAI
The flexibility and resilience people show, even if they have to live in a city with such density, chaos, and pressures on its resources. It's the more intangible things like the community feel in the old residential compounds and the slums alike, that I believe give Mumbaikars a strong sense of belonging and the strength to 'survive' the city. Without that, I feel many people would feel lost. It would be a shame if that sense of community disappears when everybody starts living in anonymous high-rise towers.

EVERY BUILDING MUST SHOUT

HAFEEZ CONTRACTOR

Hafeez Contractor (1950) earned his Graduate Diploma in Architecture from the University of Bombay, after which he completed an MS in Architecture at Columbia University in New York, in the USA. He started his career as an apprentice to his relative T. Kharaghat and became an associate partner in the latter's firm after five years.

In 1983 he started his own firm: *Architect Hafeez Contractor*. At present his firm has about 530 employees and its portfolio covers all aspects of architecture and urban planning. Projects range from hospitality to commercial spaces, and from infrastructure to retail and education campuses. He designed one of South Asia's tallest buildings: the *Imperial Towers* located in Tardeo, Mumbai. The current affairs magazine *India Today* listed him in 2003 and 2004 among India's 50 Most Powerful Indians.

'In India we have festivals that are important. And all those festivals are loud. That is my idea of how buildings should be. They should be loud! Every building must shout.'

In a labyrinthine office building in Mumbai's Fort area we speak with architect Hafeez Contractor, while sipping tea from mugs with his name on them. Loved by some, despised by others, he has not only set the standard for how commercial architecture firms operate in the city, his signature is found on much of the city's skyline. Hafeez's work does not just get imitated. 'They go beyond copying my designs', he says. 'Some literally use my name to convince clients: they advertise with it! They write in their brochure: "Like Hafeez Contractor".'

He does not mind it. His is the largest architecture firm in the city. With a team of approximately five hundred employees, he is undoubtedly Mumbai's best-known architect.

TWO HUNDRED PROJECTS

The business philosophy of Hafeez is simple. He works for anyone. 'If you pay, I play', he laughs. Then, in a more serious tone he adds: 'Why should I reject clients? Am I a madman? I believe in relationships and in building for the future. You know what it is? I would reject a project if I dislike a person, because I don't want to work with people I don't like. But as it is, I rarely dislike people.'

The result is an impressive portfolio. It is large, very large. It is not uncommon for him to work on two hundred projects at the same time. And at times he has worked on four hundred simultaneously as well. Although he works with a large staff, and although for each project there are several architects on board, he claims he personally oversees each project himself. How he manages to take on so many projects at the same time is 'by keeping things simple'. 'Our practice is different', he explains. 'It is not like other practices. We work with a small team on one product. We are constantly looking how to simplify things. The client could have a project manager. I will give him one page. If he says he wants 1000 pages, I'll tell him there is no need for that.'

COMPETITION

The hectic work pace in Mumbai does not deter Hafeez. Nor does he fear competition, not from Indian firms, and not from foreign architects or architecture firms. 'Go send them to work here', he challenges us. 'But do know: the clients want everything overnight. They give you a job today, and they want the design tomorrow. It doesn't matter if you are sick, if your tummy aches. You have got to deliver.' To illustrate this he shares: 'I signed a project for one hundred five-star hotels yesterday. They gave me the requirements. We talked about it. And then their deadline came: the date they gave me is five weeks from now! You have to deliver fast, on the spot almost. In fact, I sketched the outline for them during the meeting itself.' To prove this he pulls the sketch out of his pocket and shows us what he drew.

HORSES AND GRANNIES

Hafeez is clear about it: to run a firm like he does, he expects the full dedication and commitment of his staff. 'The staff is essentially divided into two teams: our "horses" and "grannies". The horses started here as trainees. They are the young guys. They are flexible, and have no obligations at home. They work hard and with dedication. If they stay on, they become the new grannies: the ones who will look over the shoulder of the new horses. They provide advice and ensure that the little details of a project are attended to.' The firm has also had foreign trainees but found that they generally only stay for five to six months. 'They don't stick, because they are unable to handle the pressure.'

STYLE

He might be the number one in terms of projects, and responsible for what much of what the new skyline of Mumbai looks like, but he has yet to receive critical acclaim from his peers. When confronted with the rather negative appraisal of his work by most local and international architects Hafeez says: 'In the eyes of architects I do bad work, but it is work that I am very proud of. I don't think it is bad work. People may say they don't like my buildings, but they have to look at the circumstances, the budget, and the timeline under which a project was done as well. If all that is considered I would get distinction everywhere!'

Ultimately this distinction is not what he seems to be after. He does not want to satisfy architects, but rather his clients and himself. 'A lot of projects I did are townships in neoclassical style. Yes, architects hate it. I love it. And you know, architects are never going to be my clients. I do my work, and as an architect you are supposed to cater to a vast, wide spectrum of people. I am not here to please architects. I have to satisfy poor people and rich people. I have to make buildings from 1000 square metres to 100,000 square metres. Buildings that work, and that my costumers and I like.'

SUCCES

'Many people ask me what I deem my most successful project and expect me to answer that it was the residential houses for rich clients that I did. But in fact, building something like that does not give me any pleasure. Because the budget is not a problem, land is not a problem, time is not a problem, nothing is a problem. A fool can make a nice structure under those conditions! If someone comes to me and says, "I want a building tomorrow. I want it on this small plot of 800 square metres, and my budget is half of what you normally charge", and I make something successful and nice... Well, that would be a great project and become my personal favorite building.'

LEARNING FROM...

He has a clear idea on what the rest of the world can learn from Mumbai: to be frugal with both space and resources. 'I feel we in India do our work in a most economic manner. We don't overbuild. We live very frugally. If not for India, and for Africa, I don't know where the whole world will go.' He points out that Indians take up less space per person, and use fewer resources than people in the West. 'I don't know what the size of an average house is in the West. Seventy square metres maybe? A hundred? Here, having twenty-five square metres for five people is called a luxury. I don't want to say that this is the best way of living, but it is sure that we are not wasting money like the West. They are wasting everything, the resources of whole world. They have been wasting and they are still doing it.'

FUTURE

Although Hafeez feels a lot has changed in the architectural practice of Mumbai, and although he emphasizes that it has become tougher and tougher, as competition has increased and with the amount of work slowing down as at present, he is not worried about the future. 'Life is great for architects in India it seems. But let me be clear. We have survived. Right up to 1995 there was hardly any construction going on in this country. Everyone went abroad. People told me I was a fool when I came back from America. The grass hasn't always been green. And look at where we are now! There is so much to do in India. We are 110 crore [1 crore is 10 million] people. The world population is 700 crore. We are one-seventh of the world. We have to house more people, more people need an office. We need more education, more health facilities. So much work has to be done.'

BUCKLEY COURT, COLABA

THE IMPERIAL TWIN TOWERS, TARDEO

HIRANANDANI GARDENS, POWAI

THE GATEWAY OF INDIA, APOLLO BUNDER

MY MUMBAI
HAFEEZ CONTRACTOR

MUMBAI IS SPECIAL BECAUSE
It is such a small city, yet housing so many people. I think that is the best way of living: in dense cities. We have an area of 430 square kilometres on which this city is build. Of that, 120 square kilometres is used as the National Park. Another 20 is taken up by mangrove forests, and yet another 30 by railway land. If we deduct all these things only 150 square kilometres remains for the people to live. And we still need to deduct the roads, commercial buildings, municipal and other government buildings etc., etc. And what you are left with is a small area where 18 million people live happily ever after. What more do you want?

MY FAVOURITE LANDMARK
Of course the first landmarks that come to mind are the *Victoria Terminus* [*Chhatrapati Shivaji Terminus*], the *Taj Mahal Hotel* and the *Gateway of India*. But to me the real landmark of the city is not a particular building or structure, but the achievements of those people who built their lives here from scratch; the millions of people who came to Mumbai without any documents or protection and who started living and started earning here. They may have started as pavement dwellers and now graduated to a house. The slums they live in, those are landmark buildings for the city, I feel. I am not saying they are good things. No, they are unfortunate. But they are Mumbai landmarks nevertheless.

THE BEST PLACE TO RELAX
That is my home, and in particular one seat near the window from where I can observe the trees outside. I find it amazing that if you look at a trunk longer, that you will find a lot of activity taking place in it. Thousands of things are happening on the tree, it is a city by itself.

IF ONE THING COULD BE DEMOLISHED IT WOULD BE
At present... nothing. If I was a sheikh, I would say take out all the asbestos and replace it with silver coated wood or so. But within this context, there are other priorities: there is a guy who doesn't have clothes, another who doesn't have a proper lunch during the day, and yet another who doesn't have a toilet or running water. So for now... let the asbestos be there. Because for the time being it is doing its purpose, and when the time is right we deal with it. Now giving water, food and a toilet to all in the city is a priority.

WHAT WE CAN LEARN FROM MUMBAI
How to be efficient with space and resources. In so many cities in the world about 30 to 40 percent of the land is used for public transport. Yet, if you see how much time it still takes to go from one part of the city to another part... In Mumbai about 11 or 12 percent of the surface is built up with roads. Look at the amount of money allocated and spent on public transport in this city and how much time it takes from one part to the other part of the city. I think if you compare these facts and figures from Mumbai with other cities, you will come up with exemplary numbers. Numbers and budgets the rest of the world can learn from.

Unfortunately, it is more popular to emphasize the bad numbers, the numbers that seem to show how much we are suffering. But what I want to underline is to imagine how many people in this city are not suffering and are enjoying life. Instead of the 60 people that the train carriages are designed for, they carry 400 persons during peak hour. How can you stand straight in a congested area like that? How can you commute like that every day, smell someone's armpit, and be happy also? That is what people in the world can learn from Mumbai.

HOUSING 100,000 PEOPLE AT A TIME

ARUN, SUSHMA AND SALONI DEODHAR

Arun Deodhar (1949), originally from Pune, completed his B.Arch at Bombay University in 1981. After working in Germany for several years he set up his own architecture and interior design office in Mumbai, *Deodhar Associates*. At present the firm employs forty-five people. He works together with his wife, Sushma Deodhar, and his daughter, Saloni Deodhar.

Sushma Deodhar (1958) received her B.Arch in 1983 from Bombay University. She started her career with *Great India Metal Industries*, but soon established her own furniture factory in Nasik. In 1995 she moved to Mumbai and focused on architectural projects, in particular in relation to slum rehabilitation in Mumbai. In recent years she pursued a PhD at the University of Mumbai in addition to her work as an architect. In 2012 she successfully defended her thesis entitled *Management in Real Estate in India and Abroad*.

Saloni Deodhar (1986) graduated from KRVIA in Mumbai in 2010 and joined *Deodhar Associates* in the same year. Thanks to an exchange programme she gained international experience as a student at Bern University of Applied Sciences in Switzerland. She extended her stay abroad for seven months by taking up a position as an intern (*praktikant*) in Bern with architecture and urban planning firm *Itten+Brechbühl*.

Deodhar is a thirty-year-old family-run architecture firm. Husband and wife Arun and Sushma Deodhar and their daughter Saloni Deodhar have, over the years, built an impressive portfolio of work in and around Mumbai. We meet all three of them in a residential building in Vile Parle where their office is located. We listen to their experiences and scrutinize the designs hanging on their office walls and depicted in their brochures. Very soon we realize that *Deodhar* may be a unique firm in Mumbai's architectural landscape: they wear a commercial and a social hat at the same time.

REHABILITATION AND REDEVELOPMENT

A large number of *Deodhar*'s designs are essentially for housing projects: the rehabilitation of slums and the redevelopment of old buildings. 'There are no free plots', Sushma Deodhar explains. 'All the land in Mumbai is already built up, and all we can do in this city is redeveloping and rehabilitating.' As a result she labels their task as architects as 'going from estate to real estate'.

Sushma knows what she is talking about as she recently defended her PhD thesis at the University of Mumbai on the subject of 'real estate management in India and abroad'. Part of her study focused on slums and slum redevelopment. This, in combination with the importance of slum rehabilitation projects in Deodhar's portfolio, leads to our conversation returning again and again to this fascinating aspect of designing residential architecture in Mumbai.

SLUMS IN MUMBAI

How important slum rehabilitation is in Mumbai becomes clear simply from a look at the numbers: more than half of Mumbai's 12.5 million inhabitants live in slums. In Mumbai, the slum dwellings are not necessarily made from the typical waste material that comes to mind when one hears the word 'slum'. They are often made of stone, and many slums are like villages themselves; many are over thirty years old, and some even much older. Yet what all slums have in common is that residents generally have inadequate access to safe water and sanitation. On top of that, they live in extremely overcrowded houses and densely populated areas, and lack security in their residential status. All in all enough reason to seek solutions for better housing.

FROM DEMOLITION TO REHABILITATION

After a period when slums were merely demolished, the Maharashtra state government, from the 1970s onwards, began slum improvement by trying to regularize and control slum colonies. 'In the 1990s special provisions were made for slum redevelopment', Sushma Deodhar explains, 'but these failed miserably. The government delivered too late, the quality of the structures they put up was bad. There was rampant corruption. The projects lacked in participation of the slum dwellers and overall there was a complete lack of transparency.' After this failure, the government decided to pull out of active slum rehabilitation and to give itself the role of regulator rather than developer. 'They found that developers can provide something that the government cannot', Sushma says.

At present several departments are involved in various aspects of slum rehabilitation (i.e. the Housing and Urban Development departments of the Maharashtra state government, the Maharashtra Housing and Development Authority (MHADA) and the municipal government (MCGM)). However, the most important body since 1996 is the Slum Rehabilitation Authority (SRA). 'The SRA was conceived and operates as the authority where developers go for "one-window clearance" of their slum rehabilitation proposals', Sushma explains.

SLUM REHABILITATION: THE RULES

So how does it work? 'First of all, you need to find an eligible slum. That is, a slum that existed on January 1, 1995 or before that', Sushma starts, taking us through the most important rules. 'Next, slum dwellers can come together to form a society for implementation of the rehabilitation scheme. Or an NGO can take the initiative, or a commercial developer.' Irrespective of who takes the initiative, the rehabilitation can only start when the inhabitants approve of it. 'You can only rehabilitate a slum, after taking the slum dwellers consent', Sushma explains. Eligible slum dwellers, those who can prove they moved to the slum prior to 1995, have to sign a consent form. This is the case even if the plot is owned by a private party. 'Simply being the owner of the land no longer gives you the power to clear the slum and start building.' To get this consent the developer selects local people in the slum itself to convince the others. Sushma: 'You need the help of maybe six-seven people. By convincing or force, or any other way, he will take the signatures of the people.' Sushma illustrates that this first step can take a long time, and is not straightforward. 'In one case we started 12 years back to take consent. And each time there is Ganesh Chaturti [Ganesh festival] or Holi, all the builders need to pay the slum dwellers again...'

After having obtained the required consent and the project is given the go-ahead, the slum dwellers are given notice to vacate the land. 'Unless part of the plot is already empty this means you have to wait again. Slum dwellers get eleven months time to vacate the land and move into transit camps', says Sushma.

SQUARE METRES & FSI

'Under the current scheme you can rehabilitate a slum, provided you give a "self-contained tenement" with a minimum carpet area of 25 square metres to the slum dwellers free of cost. You also need to give back the same amount of recreation spaces as was there before, with a minimum of 8 percent of the entire area. And you have to provide structures for communal facilities such as a *balwadi* [crèche], a society office, a welfare centre etc.', Sushma says. 'In return, the government grants the builder permission to sell the proportionate of built-up space in the open market.' 'What is particularly interesting', Arun adds, 'is that an FSI [Floor Space Index] up to 3 or 4 can be allowed at this type of site, whereas 1.33/1.00 FSI is available for non-slum sites.'

HANUMAN NAGAR

Deodhar, over the years, did more than fifty such slum rehabilitation projects. Without doubt their grandest is *Hunaman Nagar*, in Kandivali (E). Quite literally so. 'It is a 125-acre (50 ha) plot where approximately 25,000 slum tenants were located. That makes it one of the vastest government slum clearances under the Slum Redevelopment Scheme ever. 'Our plan has 14,319 flats for rehabilitation tenants, and the same area of flats will be put up for sale', Sushma says, while showing us the model images. When completed, the complex will house over 100,000 people. Saloni explains: 'With slum rehabilitation the idea is to fit a maximum number of people in a minimum amount of space. But at the same time we tried to keep an eye on the quality of living. We designed a building of sixteen stories to house all these people. Normally slum redevelopment buildings are seven stories high, because lower buildings are easier to maintain. In this project, by making the buildings higher, we are able to house more people, and provide more open spaces. Every cluster has its own garden and there is a big communal garden. We thought about providing gardens on different levels, or even vertically. But the rules do not approve of that.'

The project is currently under construction and planned to be fully finished by 2020.

REDEVELOPMENT

As empty plots are hardly available in the island city and suburbs of Mumbai, many architects are essentially involved in redevelopment. Sometimes an old building is renovated, but more often the old structure is demolished, and a new one built. The new building gives the original residents larger apartments, and generally has extra flats that the builder puts up for sale. Ideally, both the residents and the developer profit from the redevelopment.

When we ask about the differences of working on slum rehabilitation and housing redevelopment Sushma shares: 'In some ways redevelopment of a housing society is easier than a slum. Because generally the people are more educated. But in other ways it is harder, because of the attachment people have to their area, their building. Maybe their buildings are in a bad shape, but they value that attachment a lot.' Sushma emphasizes, however, that in both cases the architect requires patience. 'Lots of patience, as large-scale projects, be it rehabilitation or redevelopment can and will take as long as twenty years from inception to completion.'

PROJECT MANAGEMENT CONSULTANT

Any housing society in Mumbai that is interested in redevelopment needs to appoint a project management consultant (PMC). 'This is compulsory now for housing societies that wish to redevelop', Arun says. *Deodhar* offers this service to housing societies and is involved in several housing projects not as the prime architect or developer, but as the PMC.

'As the project management consultant of a housing society we first make a feasibility report with all the details of the building and the plot and some general calculations. In the report we explain to the residents everything that is viable, what they can demand and cannot demand. And of course we tell them how much extra should be asked', says Sushma, smiling.

The next step is to assist in the tendering stage. 'As we work in the interest of the society, we help with recommending which developer is suitable, depending on their credentials in terms of eligibility, and based on the maximum benefit to the society.' In practice, however, they often work in close cooperation with a particular developer from the beginning. 'During an information meeting we give a presentation to the residents. Our job then is often to try and educate them. We tell them what the benefits are of a new house. The developer and architect together try to convince them. Jointly we do that', Arun says.

Once the selection of the developer is definitive, a detailed plan is made. *Deodhar* in its role as PMC helps with this too. And finally, during the construction phase, they supervise the quality of the construction work.

LEARNING FOR...

From Sushma's presentation, and the experiences the family members share on working in Mumbai, we get the impression that knowing the rules and regulations, the laws and by-laws, are crucial for anyone who wants to successfully engage in rehabilitation and redevelopment projects in Mumbai. We ask Arun Deodhar if this impression is correct. He agrees. But he emphasizes that this does not disqualify young foreign architects from the Indian market. 'Not at all', he argues, 'the Indian student also doesn't know about the rules and regulations and has to learn most of them on the job!' He adds: 'Neither do Indian graduates know much about sizes for residential buildings. They don't know how to design a 2BHK [two bedrooms, hall & kitchen] apartment. As of yet, they don't learn much about residential building. Instead they get assignments in college like "Make me something on this 2 acre plot". Oh yes, that is good for your imagination, but in a lifetime you probably will not get such an assignment in Mumbai!'

Arun explains how in Mumbai standard sizes of apartments depend on the area where they will be built. 'Fresh out of school the students are unaware of this, but between Borivali and Andheri a 140 square metre apartment is slightly luxurious. Between Andheri and Vile Parle a 110 square metre flat is sold as luxurious. And between Vile Parle and Khar the same goes for a 90 square metre residential space.' Arun feels that it is important that students in India to learn about these differences and, about the differences between lower, middle and upper-class houses. He feels that architecture schools' curricula would improve if students were also to learn *for* Mumbai.

LEARNING FROM...

As *Deodhar* has worked extensively both with the government and with private developers, we want to know what we can learn from their experience. Arun needs not think twice about his answer. Resolutely he states: 'The relation between the architect and the private developers is friendly and professional. The government lacks in that. Payments always come late for example. With the government you don't get your money. With private developers you know you will get it today or tomorrow. The government procedure is so lengthy and complicated in all stages that you might have to pay a bribe to get your expected fees in time.' In other words, Arun would advise those starting in the Indian market to work with private firms rather than government organizations.

HANUMAN NAGAR CHS, KANDIVALI

PROPOSED LAYOUT
ANUMAN NAGAR

HANUMAN NAGAR CHS, KANDIVALI

RESIDENTIAL COMPLEX BUILT UNDER THE SLUM REDEVELOPMENT SCHEME, KANDIVALI

MY MUMBAI

SUSHMA DEODHAR

MUMBAI IS SPECIAL BECAUSE

Mumbai is the commercial capital of India. That is the reason it has become a magnetic city which attracts the people from not only neighbouring states, but from all over India to earn their bread and butter. Being part of a tropical country, the weather is moderate in all seasons, which makes the city comfortable to live in. The people from all over India who want to stay in Mumbai get the work of their choice. Anybody and everybody who comes to work here gets an accommodation, whether it is formal apartments or in informal settlements [slums].

THIS CAN BE IMPROVED

There is an overload of population, and that can be improved by enhancing the accommodation capacity of Mumbai. Since there are no open plots that can be developed as residential accommodation, redevelopment, and exploiting the Floor Space Index potential of a built-up plots, is the only solution.

MY FAVOURITE PLACE

Bandra Bandstand, a recently built promenade along the seafront in the western suburb of Bandra. It is a kilometre long and attracts lots of people throughout the day, but in particular during the evenings.

MY FAVOURITE RESTAURANT

Gajalee in Vile Parle. An amazing place where you get the best and freshest fish of all Mumbai.

MY FAVOURITE LANDMARK

Any railway station. It becomes a transient landmark or rather it becomes a landmark while you are in transit through the city. Mumbai has a great system of suburban railways with almost 150 stations along its rails. The business district in the most southern tip of the island is connected via fast and slow local trains to stations as far away as 60 kilometres. More than 7 million people use the trains in the city any given day.

THE BEST PLACE TO RELAX

Juhu Beach. Mumbai is blessed with a long coastline and a series of beaches. *Juhu Beach* is one of my favourite places to relax. I can sit there and feel the sea breeze after a long and strenuous day.

IF ONE THING COULD BE DEMOLISHED IT WOULD BE

MHADA Transit Camp in Bandra (E). MHADA stands for Maharashtra Housing and Area Development Authority. This state authority, all over Mumbai, has built over fifty so-called transit camps. Most of these buildings were built before 1940 and have been poorly maintained. Many of its current residents are people who moved to these buildings from the 1970s onwards thinking this would be temporary housing for them. Their houses were undergoing redevelopment and they expected to return to their old neighbourhood as soon as the redevelopment project of their building was completed. In reality, many were unable to return and were 'stuck' in the dilapidated transit camp buildings. Redevelopment was often delayed, if not cancelled because of infrastructure projects taking up the space where their old home was, or because zoning laws and litigation stalled the projects.

MY CHOICE OF TRANSPORTATION

Two-wheeler. It is the fastest mode of transport through the city nowadays.

WHAT WE CAN LEARN FROM MUMBAI

Mumbai is one of the biggest cities in world. Whoever wants to work, will find work over here. No human being in Mumbai sleeps with an empty stomach at night. Mumbai has the courage to face any natural or man-made calamity at any time. It has an enormous pace and can start its daily routine immediately after such kind of shocks.

ORGANIC FARMING IN THE CONCRETE JUNGLE

ADRIENNE THADANI

Adrienne Thadani (1987) is the founder and director of an urban farming initiative in Mumbai. Adrienne, half-Indian, half-American, was born and raised in Washington DC. She graduated in the Humanities from the University of Michigan, Ann Arbor in 2008 with a degree in Arts and Ideas, focusing on Subaltern Studies. She moved to India shortly after. She started *Fresh & Local* in 2010, in response to the lack of fresh, organic, locally grown produce in the city, and the lack of urban farming resources available. She is passionate about community activism and human rights, specifically relating to public health and nutrition. In 2011, Adrienne joined Columbia University's *Studio X Mumbai*, an open space for collaborative work and exchange of ideas relating to the future of urban areas and the built environment. She currently works at *Studio X* and runs *Fresh & Local* with five other team members.

Over the past two years Adrienne Thadani, through her organization *Fresh & Local*, has taught over four hundred people in Mumbai how to start an urban farm on their own balconies and roofs. She also started several urban farms in the city. Her work has added to the availability of organic produce, and the greening of the city. It has added extra space to the city as well, by developing new functions for otherwise unused areas. After visiting two of her farms, we meet her at a hip café in Bandra to find out more about her journey, her plans for the future, and what she has learned from Mumbai.

FROM WEDDING PLANNING TO HORTICULTURE

It was the wish to reconnect with her Indian family and father's city that brought Adrienne Thadani to Mumbai in 2009. 'At home, in Washington DC, I had been making and selling Obama T-shirts during his first presidential campaign. I wasn't sure what to do next, and thought it was a good time to go to Mumbai for a while. I had a wonderful time and didn't have to think long when a Mumbai friend asked, after I returned to the US, to come back to Mumbai and help plan her wedding. With the little money I had left I bought a one-way ticket to Mumbai, and I have been here ever since.'

In addition to wedding planning Adrienne occupied herself with an office job at her friend's real estate and landscaping company. 'One day, while going around the different departments to collect material for a presentation I was preparing on eco-friendly practices, I walked into their horticulture department. I immediately loved the atmosphere there. So I asked them if I could shadow them and ask questions, to learn about plants, soil and gardening in India.' The enthusiasm she encountered turned out to be crucial for her future in Mumbai. The wedding concluded, Adrienne realized she wanted to do something with the knowledge of plants, gardens and farming she had now acquired.

TOXIC SPINACH

Her first motivation to create urban farms was to find a solution to the lack of organic food available. 'I was surprised when I heard many people do not eat spinach anymore in the city. They complain it is grown by the train tracks and heavily polluted and they urged me to stop eating it as well. But all it did was make me wonder: "Why is there no alternative available in a city this size? Why is there is no organic section in the supermarket, no farmers market, no local farmer I can go to myself to get non-toxic spinach?" I decided I didn't want to be merely complaining, I wanted to find a real solution.'

When she first pitched her ideas she found very little support. 'The NGOs I approached did not consider this development work, and told me to do something else, like build toilets. Others told me to use my time and energy to teach children English', Adrienne remembers. 'The people from the horticulture department said I would have to start on my own, but that they would help me. And they did. They helped me figure out how I could create a farm on a rooftop or on a balcony in this climate and with local resources.'

BALCONY FARMS AND WORKSHOPS

The first step was starting a simple herb garden on her friend's balcony. After that she set to work at *Bombay Hub* (now *Bombay Connect*): a shared office space for social entrepreneurs in Bandra. 'The moment we started putting plants on the empty balcony there, people started using it. And when they saw the plants were not just decoration but also producing tomatoes, cucumbers and fragrant herbs, they got more interested and started asking me questions: "What do you do? How do you do that?"', Adrienne recalls.

'The *Hub* manager suggested I organize a workshop to explain all of it. The moment I announced it ten people signed up, and I had to start a waiting list. Clearly this was something people had been waiting for! By now I have organized over thirty workshops, and introduced some five hundred people to urban farming through workshops and events.'

Her success has negated the image that organic farming 'only works in the West'. 'More press coverage on the downsides of pesticide usage and the emergence of a farmers market and organic groceries has also lead to an increased demand for "clean foods"', Adrienne thinks. 'In India the motivation for people to start their own farm or to buy local products is not about reducing the human footprint or about larger environmental concerns. The main motivation is health concerns, of themselves and their families.'

FLYOVER FARM

One of the biggest projects Adrienne worked on is the *Flyover Farm*: a rooftop farm, so named as it overlooks the flyover above Mohammed Ali Road. She started this project together with Nicola Antaki, a British friend and architect living in Mumbai. 'The owner of the building wanted to set up a herb garden on the roof', Adrienne says. 'When she took me and Nicola to the site, it was clear that we could do so much more with the space! Many chats and brainstorming sessions later she offered us the whole space to start a rooftop community farm.'

The next step was to generate enough funds to buy the necessary tools, soil, seeds, and materials, like crates and pots. But also to hire labour and transport means to get soil from one end of the city to the other, and up on the roof. Adrienne twice received a grant for social entrepreneurship from *UnLtd India*. 'Aside from the monetary support, the first year with them really helped me further develop my ideas. But for the *Flyover Farm* we had to find extra funding and we decided to use *kickstarter.com*, a crowdfunding platform. We wanted to put the idea out there and see if other people too felt this was a good initiative. Nicola made beautiful designs and illustrations for our campaign. It worked and we received our seed capital.'

FROM FARMING TO OPEN SPACES

Adrienne and Nicola started working on the farm after the monsoon ended. They invested in various fruit trees, and planted vegetables like gourds, spinach, *bhindi* (a.k.a. okra), and carrots, as well as various herbs such as coriander, mint, fenugreek, and curry leaf. They invited residents and other volunteers to help construct the garden. The produce will be sold at market rates to the residents of the building. The surplus will be sold to the neighbouring vegetable vendors on the street.

Providing the residents and the neighbourhood with pesticide-free vegetables, herbs and fruits, and showing the rest of the city that it is possible to farm on their own roof or balcony without damaging the building, are, however, no longer the only aims of the farm. Adrienne and Nicola realized that their project had become something bigger than that. 'It became a public space project', Adrienne says. 'Before we started, the roof was an unused space. There was no shade, nothing to see, and no reason to come up there. Now the roof has multiple purposes, multiple functions. It produces food, but it has also become a playground. It is a wonderful place for children to safely run around. It has even become a space where class barriers are broken: the children from low-income families who live in the building meet and play with children from other social strata who come along with their parents to volunteer in the garden.'

The roof became a meeting point for the older residents as well. 'They drink tea together and take a morning walk in a beautiful traffic-free space', Adrienne explains. 'When we realized the roof had gotten multiple functions we decided to include a walking path in our design and make more shaded areas where people can gather. In the weekends there are yoga sessions and other activities for residents and for outsiders.'

LEARNING FROM...

Throughout our conversation Adrienne emphasizes that the city has taught her to look at the world in a different way. She feels that one of the most important lessons was 'to go with the flow'. 'None of the projects I did would have been there had I stuck to a straight plan. I know that if I had come with one fixed idea of what to achieve, I would simply not have done all I am doing now', she says. 'What you can learn from Mumbai is to have a vision, to have a dream, and to be flexible enough to realize it in different ways.'

FUTURE PLANS

Despite the success she's had so far, generating sufficient funding remains a challenge. But it doesn't stop Adrienne from developing new ideas. Together with Nicola she is working on a replicable *Pop-Up Garden*, teaming up with a fine dining restaurant in the city to supply them with fresh produce. She also dreams about making a central composting site in the city, where kitchen-waste is used to sustain a surrounding garden.

Adrienne realizes she will need to buckle down for the long haul, and will no doubt have to conquer more scepticism along the way. But luckily she has shown in the past years that this won't keep her from dreaming, nor from realizing projects that aim to make the city a more beautiful and more liveable space.

A FRESH & LOCAL Project For more information please visit wwwfreshandlocalorg Fresh and Local is an urban farming initiative in Mumbai, India Illustration by NKA

THE FLYOVER FARM

CRAWFORD MARKET

MY MUMBAI
ADRIENNE THADANI

MUMBAI IS SPECIAL BECAUSE
So much in this city doesn't work, yet still the city works, it functions everyday, almost against the odds. It can be quite frustrating, and it makes you want to make things better. But the amazing part is that often it just takes a few tweaks here and there and you are able to make huge improvements.

THIS CAN BE IMPROVED
Traffic, by improving public transport. Trains and buses need to become a more attractive and practical alternative to relieve the strain on the city's streets. The public transport figures in India are inflated as rickshaws and taxis are counted as public transport, which of course they aren't.

Making the existing public transport more user-friendly, and improving awareness about routes and timetables, could make it easier for those who now take taxis and rickshaws or their own car to consider using mass transit. When I lived in South Mumbai, I would take the bus to work and to visit family, but I only knew how to do it because someone showed me how. Without that guidance it would have taken me a lot longer to do so. Similarly, I first took the train with a friend, who explained to me all the details. Once you start using the buses and trains it becomes easy, and part of your daily life. But for many people coming to this city, it is very hard to figure out the transit system, and people get very discouraged. For example, some friends thought the bus numbers were only in Hindi, not realizing that the English numbers are written on the side of the bus. Or others don't know how to get a train pass or about train coupons. Without a doubt there are many features of the public transport that must be improved, such as quality of stations, frequency of trains, handicap accessibility, safety – and the list goes on – but that said, better signage and clear information explaining how to use the existing facilities would help in the interim.

MY FAVOURITE PLACE
That would be *Marine Drive*, and in particular the Art Deco buildings lining it. I like them even more now that I have seen the same type of districts in Cuba and in Miami. There I am reminded of Mumbai, and here of those other places.

MY FAVOURITE RESTAURANT
For South Indian food I love going to *Café Madras* in Matunga. For North Indian Punjabi food *Papa Panchos* in Pali Naka, Bandra is a favourite. And for Indian snacks like *pani puri* it has to be *Kailash Parbat* in Colaba and Bandra.

MY FAVOURITE LANDMARK
The *Taj Mahal Hotel* and the *Gateway of India* in Colaba. My dad grew up just around the corner and as a little kid we used to walk around that area. I love that neighbourhood, to see the water, the open space at the *Gateway*, even the guys with the big balloons. They all bring back very fond memories of my childhood.

THE BEST PLACE TO RELAX
The *Breach Candy Club*.

IF ONE THING COULD BE DEMOLISHED IT WOULD BE
The entire *Bandra Kurla Complex*. I am so over this idea of an office park with box-like buildings and glass windows. I think the construction of that park is a prime example of a missed opportunity. They had so much space to make a really nice new neighbourhood. Instead they made a dead area with massive spaces between persons on the street and buildings and with bike lanes that do not go anywhere and are not protected from the other traffic.

MY CHOICE OF TRANSPORTATION
The local trains. Despite the fact that they could be improved, it is still the fastest way to get around in Mumbai.

WHAT WE CAN LEARN FROM MUMBAI
Don't rush. Anything is possible... if you have time.

A NEW LIGHT ON MUMBAI

BAS LOSEKOOT

Bas Losekoot (1979) studied Graphic Design at the Grafisch Lyceum Amsterdam, Photography at the Royal Academy of Art in The Hague, and also studied at the Netherlands Film Academy in Amsterdam. His work has been exhibited in museums, libraries and at photo festivals in the Netherlands and the United States.

While still a student he was nominated for one of the most prestigious Dutch photography awards, the *Silver Camera*. In the years thereafter the list of nominations and awards grew; he bagged the *Silver Camera Award* in the category Foreign Documentary in 2011.

Bas has done numerous assignments for Dutch, Belgian and German magazines, and created commercials and advertisements. His passion, however, is documentary photography. In his current project, called *The Urban Millennium Project*, he aims to capture life in the world's largest cities through his lens. After spending a month each in New York, São Paulo and Seoul, he visited Mumbai in October 2012. In 2013 and 2014 he will visit Shanghai, Mexico City, London and Tokyo. The eight city photo documentaries thus created will result in a single publication capturing the essence of twenty-first century urbanisms.

Bas Losekoot has worked in studios and on movie sets and in recent years began to focus on street photography. 'A year ago I realized I could *combine* these disciplines and started to view the world as a studio', he explains. 'I started to view the people through my lens as actors and the street as their theatre. Just like one would do on a movie set, I use extra lights on the street. I add artificial light to natural light.'

URBAN MILLENNIUM PROJECT

With this technique Bas started travelling the world to photograph people who work and live in its many metropolises and document the fact that, for the first time in history, more people live in cities than in rural areas. He called it *The Urban Millennium Project.* 'I want to explore human behaviour in this urban context. Who are the residents of the world's largest cities? How do they cope among the masses? How do they interact with each other? What can we see if we "freeze" their movements? What do their facial expressions and their poses in these unguarded moments tell us about their city, about humanity, about the urban fabric? Are urbanites the same worldwide, and if not, what differences are there?'

LOCATIONS

Bas selected eight cities (New York, São Paulo, Seoul, London, Mexico City, Tokyo, Shanghai and Mumbai) based on their population size and density, the speed of their growth, and their geographical spread around the world. But how does he choose his locations *within* the cities? 'That selection is determined by the wish to capture areas that characterize a city', says Bas. 'In Mumbai – a city with one of the highest densities of the world – I tried to find places where many people gather, where people, quite literally, scramble for a place to stand and walk and can't help but bump into each other.'

'Finding those locations starts even before I board the plane', Bas continues. 'I scrutinize *Google Earth* and try to locate the city centre. In New York that is rather easy: go to where the tall buildings are, and you will find pedestrian traffic. In Mumbai that turned out to be more challenging, as I couldn't rely on what maps told me. The city's new tall buildings may be in the Bandra Kurla Complex, and half a million people may go to an office there every day, but when I reached there it seemed deserted. In Mumbai I needed to walk around more than in other cities to find the best locations and enquire among locals what the best spots would be.'

24 DAYS, 500 PICTURES A DAY

'Lots of pedestrian traffic happens at the railway stations and throughout the day in the old business district, Fort. I spent many days there, immersing myself among the people that commute to their offices. But I also ventured out to other areas: to Bandra and Lower Parel, to see how people behave in newer areas, outside of the colonial architecture and street plans.'

After scouting locations for a few days, he started photographing. 'Twenty-four days I took photographs, five hundred per day. In the end I select some twenty-odd photographs for the series. It always remains a mystery on which days I take the perfect photo.'

FACT VERSUS FICTION

'My point of departure is that I want to approach reality, but – because of the way I work – it is fiction that I produce', Bas says. 'But there are many writers who argue that only *through* fiction you can find reality and truth, that you can "lie the truth". And that is what I believe too, and what I attempt to do.'

As a photographer Bas wants to remain invisible, fly-on-the-wall style. In Mumbai this was harder to achieve than in other cities he worked in. 'Passers-by would look straight into my lens. They did not hide themselves behind sunglasses and headphones; they did not look away. They seemed unconcerned about their privacy. On the contrary: everyone seemed to *like* having his or her picture taken.'

'It was exhilarating to be so much in touch with a city and its people, but it had downsides too', he adds. 'It made it hard to get photos from which I am really absent. Frankly, I am still not entirely sure if it wouldn't be more truthful if I'd include those where people look straight in the lens, making contact with the photographer hiding behind it, as it is part of what Mumbai *is*.'

ARRIER
करिअर

'बी' विभाग
स्वागत करीत आहे
WEL COME
TO 'B' WARD

MUMBAI-27

देवनारायण

ARCHITECTURE EDUCATION AS A KEY TO APPROPRIATE DEVELOPMENT

RAJIV MISHRA

Rajiv Mishra (1966) gained his General Diploma in Architecture from the Academy of Architecture in Bombay. Subsequently he studied Town and Country Planning at the Government College of Engineering in Pune, pursued a post-graduate diploma in Urban Management at the Institute of Housing Studies in Rotterdam, in the Netherlands and completed a post-graduate course in Management of Education at the University of Mumbai.

He has worked and continues to work on residential and commercial projects as a practising architect and consultant, and has undertaken various research studies. His research interests are issues dealing with urbanism, community architecture, heritage conservation, and bridging the gap between education and practice.

Throughout his career, Rajiv Mishra has focused the majority of his time on lecturing at architecture institutes in Mumbai. His affiliation to the Sir J.J. College of Architecture dates back to 1995, when he joined as a Visiting Lecturer. After holding several other teaching and administrative positions, he was appointed Principal in 2007, a post he still holds today.

The Sir J.J. College of Architecture is located on a sprawling campus in South Mumbai, next to CST station. In one of the beautiful old buildings we meet the Principal of the College, Rajiv Mishra, to learn about his and other colleges in the city, exchange programmes, and the time he himself spent in Rotterdam.

SIR J.J. COLLEGE OF ARCHITECTURE

'At present Mumbai has some twenty colleges of architecture, all of which are affiliated to the University of Mumbai', Rajiv starts, outlining the current architecture education scene to us. The Sir J.J. College of Architecture was the first architecture college in Asia. The foundations of the College were laid back in 1896 when a class was started within the (then twenty-year-old) Sir J.J. College of Arts, to 'produce men with practical and useful knowledge fit to be employed in an architect's office'. In 1913 the course was expanded and evolved into a college for architecture. In 1952 the College became affiliated to the University of Bombay. 'What started as a class had become a fulltime five-year course leading to a Degree of Architecture', Rajiv says. 'Nowadays, the College offers Bachelor's and Master's courses in Architecture [B.Arch and M.Arch].' The first takes five years to complete, the second is a two-year programme. In their final years students elect a specialization. 'Students can choose between urban planning, urban design, landscape architecture, urban conversation and structure management', says Rajiv.

SCHOOLS OF THOUGHT

Why would a prospective student prefer one of the twenty colleges to the other? And what should architecture firms know when they hire graduates from the various colleges? 'One reason for students to select our college is the quality of education. Ours is considered a top college within the university, and also among the other architecture colleges,' Rajiv says. 'Every year the graduating architects of our institute are among the top five of performing students.'

Quality is not the only criterion, however, the approach of the college is important as well. 'The syllabus of all the colleges affiliated to the Bombay University is the same', Rajiv explains. 'But they all follow this curriculum in their own way. The school of thought they follow and their approach to architecture is the unique selling point of each college. Upon admission students know this, and they choose the college based on the quality of teaching and their approach. Some colleges are design-based – they would emphasize concepts more. Others are more technology-based – there the execution of a project is emphasized. Again other colleges would emphasize particular specialization areas, based on the expertise of their staff. Some have more landscape teachers, others more urban planners among their staff. Some have more practising architects, and others only teachers with a Bachelor in Architecture.'

Rajiv positions his own college in the middle of the spectrum. 'At Sir J.J. College we believe, and have always believed, in a marriage between form and function. Something might be possible construction-wise, but if it is not beautiful then it is a wrong design and it has to be changed. In that sense we have an aesthetic focus. However, if a design is pleasing the eye but it can't be utilized, it is not good enough either. Both form and function should be right, then only a design is a good design. As a result of this philosophy we place an equal emphasis on design and technology in our lectures and workshops.'

DIPLOMAS, BACHELORS & MASTERS

To gain admission to the architecture colleges in the city, students need to have completed Class XII or a Diploma course in Engineering. Before they can enrol at Sir J.J. College they also need to pass an aptitude test.

Somewhat confused by the education system, we ask Rajiv to give us some insight into whom, for instance, we would need to hire should we want to open up an architecture firm in Mumbai. 'A Diploma course is a three-year course', he explains. 'It is essentially vocational education. Students opt for a Diploma course when they do not plan to go for higher studies and would like to find a job soon. A Diploma course gives you superior skills to start working to those who graduate from twelfth class in Commerce, Science or Arts. If you start a firm here, you may hire people with a Diploma in Engineering mostly for jobs that have an engineering application. For example, if you need a civil engineer who can supervise your sites. But generally, the staff of most firms will consist of graduates or post-graduates – those who completed a BA or an MA in Architecture at one of the colleges of architecture.'

ARCHITECTURE AS A LUCRATIVE PROSPECTIVE

'A fresh graduate with a Master's degree in Architecture can expect a salary of about INR 30,000-35,000 per month when she begins her career. After completion of the Bachelor's degree programme, graduates can expect about INR 20,000-25,000 per month, while someone with a Diploma of Engineering will initially probably earn somewhere between INR 12,000 and INR 18,000. These amounts can vary somewhat, but', Rajiv adds, 'the bigger the firm they work for, the less salary that is generally paid'.

Despite these modest starting salaries, colleges of architecture have gained significantly in popularity over the years. 'There is a great demand for gaining admission to architecture colleges nowadays', Rajiv says. 'Young people see that the real estate sector is booming, and they want to participate in it. They see the economic growth, the rapid developments, and feel architecture and planning is a lucrative prospective.'

There is a downside to this expansion of opportunities for architects and planners as well, Rajiv notes. 'With these high success rates in finding jobs and developing business in the real estate sector, it has become difficult to find teachers for the architecture colleges. The money is in the market. A career outside of the college is much more profitable and that makes it very difficult for us to get good teachers. Doing both – teaching and practising architecture – is not really possible. As a result, the education sector in the city is struggling to give good quality education.'

Rajiv is worried about the repercussions this may have not just for the education in architecture, but also for the future of architecture and planning in the city as a whole. 'If you want to improve the quality and standards in the urban development sector, your emphasis should be on good quality of architecture education. I feel that if you can control that, you can control development. Architecture education is the key to the growth of appropriate development'.

LEARNING FROM... ROTTERDAM

Reflecting on his own days as a student, Rajiv tells about his time as a fellow at the Institute of Housing Studies in Rotterdam. In 1996, he went to the Netherlands to study urban management, with an emphasis on local economic development. This was an important phase of his life, Rajiv feels. 'It changed my way of thinking. It transformed me to make the right decisions and helped me to become a better architect.'

Partially it was the formal study material that made it such a rewarding experience. 'The course really helped me to understand urbanism and how it is the most significant development in any city', Rajiv says. 'With urbanism I mean quality of life. I was taught what the parameters are that need to be resolved in a city to improve the quality of living. I started to understand that they are manifold and related to the development of residential, commercial, and industrial zones, the preparation of development plans, the ratio of open spaces to the population in the city, the rent to income ratio, and the environmental sustainability of solutions applied.'

In addition, living in Rotterdam turned out to be a life-altering experience as well. 'I lived in a city that was implementing exactly what I was learning at the institute. For example, Rotterdam was redeveloping the area called Kop van Zuid when I was there. Where earlier a seaport used to be, they decided to build houses, and thereby they improved the affordable housing supply for the city's citizens. What I saw there was that urban development and housing projects should not be so much about how to provide, but about what the real needs are of a housing complex; needs in terms of amenities, commercial infrastructure, health care, education facilities etcetera. When you design and build it should not just be about providing houses, it is about the lifestyle you are able to offer. I really felt that was and is something that Mumbai can learn from Rotterdam, as urban management policies in Mumbai should be framed and reformed to the benefit of citizens.'

COOPERATION AMONG ARCHITECTURE COLLEGES

Rajiv Mishra strongly believes that exposure to the practice of architecture is an important part of a student's education. 'We can all undergo lots of education, but if you see an example of correct development with your own eyes, than you also see the deficiencies and can try to improve it. Also, when you have learned something not just from a textbook, but from experience, you will feel more confident about your ideas and your aims. In Rotterdam I saw that it is possible to give a good quality of life in a city, and to all its inhabitants, whether they are rich or poor. This has made me confident to make statements about how to go ahead here in Mumbai. I feel I can prove it now.'

There are no student exchange programmes between the various architecture colleges in Mumbai. Nor is there any intercity exchange. According to Rajiv this is because 'the syllabi we follow are so work-oriented and so tedious that there is simply too little time'. On top of that, 'the staff is not open to it'. 'The different universities have different orientations and that makes it difficult to have a positive exchange', Rajiv explains. Furthermore, the sequencing in the curriculum varies per college in such a way that it is almost impossible to find a time slot where all students can benefit equally from the exchange.

There is some interaction between the staff of the various Indian colleges though. There is a body in place where principals of architecture colleges around India meet occasionally. Within this context they discuss many topics (architecture standards, staff recruitment, administrative problems etc.), but not the teaching subjects. When we show our surprise Rajiv laughs. 'What is there to talk about? All of us think that we already are the most effective of them all!' In a more serious tone he adds quickly: 'Of course cooperation is important. I would like to see more time invested in it. I think it is time we start cooperating as architecture colleges on a regional level – North, West, South, East – and together review the education system. If we unite ourselves we can put more pressure on the government. Now that we are alone we have no voice. No official will entertain us individually.'

INTERNATIONAL EXCHANGE

Upon graduation, about thirty percent of the graduates go abroad. 'They go there for exposure, for awareness', Rajiv shares. 'That is what they lack here, and which completes their education.'

That is not to say that Sir J.J. College of Architecture does not provide any opportunities for international exchange. They do. 'Every institution, us included, is trying to build collaboration and exchange programmes with universities in the United States and the United Kingdom. We work together with Columbia University [USA], IIT Chicago [USA], and Oxford Brookes [UK]. We have done a project, for example, in which all these colleges participated. It was on sustainable urban design. Students from the foreign colleges came here, met and worked together with our students. And some of our students and staff have also visited the foreign institutes.'

This is not the only foreign exposure the new generation of Indian architects get. 'There are the more ad hoc exchanges also', Rajiv says. Our own workshop fell in that category. 'The workshops you conducted in the context of *Learning from Mumbai* provided an opportunity for our students to learn from you as well. It was another opportunity for them to get exposed to a different way of thinking about taking decisions in the urban development sector.'

LEARNING FROM...

For Rajiv the exchange programmes are really about learning from each other. When we ask what we should learn from Mumbai he shares that he particularly likes to point out Mumbai's housing solutions to his foreign guests. 'Here in Mumbai, you can view the most adequate and the most inadequate solutions for housing. It is a city of paradoxes, of extremes. There are areas, like Dharavi, where 2,000 people share one hectare of land. Just seeing this already helps you understand density of housing. I feel that Mumbai is the best example of a city laboratory where maximum experiments of housing, density, urban design and urbanization have been carried out. It is a wonderful city to learn from if you are interested. It is full of paradoxes. That's why I fully agree with Charles Correa, who once called Mumbai "a great city, but a terrible place"'.

SIR J.J. COLLEGE OF ARCHITECTURE

MY MUMBAI
RAJIV MISHRA

MUMBAI IS SPECIAL BECAUSE
The spirit of its citizens! They possess the spirit to develop, to grow, and to make things better. They have what I call a 'positive growth' mindset.

THIS CAN BE IMPROVED
The quality of life can be improved, and in particular in the field of housing. There is a lack in supply of affordable housing. The vast majority of Mumbai's population can't afford to buy a house in the city. Not because they are poor, but because of current property rates and the lack of affordable houses on the market. Most middle-class office workers can only afford to buy a house some 60 to 90 kilometres away from their office in Mumbai. I recently read that almost 5,000 police officers live in slums. These people have legal jobs, but still can't find a good place to live.

MY FAVOURITE PLACE
My own campus. The campus of Sir J.J. College of Architecture. It is located on a large plot of land in the heart of South Mumbai, near the CST station. Apart from plenty of green and open space, there are two main heritage buildings dating from the mid-nineteenth century in which classes are still held.

MY FAVOURITE RESTAURANT
Chetana. A vegetarian *thali* restaurant in Kala Ghoda. They serve delicious Marathi and Gujarati dishes.

MY FAVOURITE LANDMARK
Flora Fountain. Even though few people notice her, Flora, the Roman goddess on the statue, notices the city that develops. She is looking north, the direction in which Mumbai has always grown. Sir Bartle Frère constructed *Flora Fountain* in 1864. He wanted to create a scenic place, not unlike the Roman forums, where the citizenry could come together to discuss the future of their city. In this way *Flora Fountain* was intended to be the 'citizen's centre of the city'. From it ran a direct road to the 'civic centre of the city', the area around *Victoria Terminus* (now *Chhatrapati Shivaji Terminus*), where the government buildings were and are. Sure, citizens never gather at *Flora Fountain*, but when I think of this monument, this landmark, I think of a place that most citizens identify themselves with, even though they might not be aware of it every day. If you haven't seen *Flora Fountain* you haven't been in Mumbai.

THE BEST PLACE TO RELAX
Haji Ali, a fifteenth century mosque and tomb located in the sea at Worli 500 metres off the coast, is one of them. And the *Hanging Gardens*, on the top of Malabar Hill, is a personal favourite too. Both are beautiful places. But if I want a place with fewer people, it would definitely be *Banganga Tank*. The origins of the tank date back to the twelfth century. It is now part of the *Walkeshwar Temple Complex*, on Malabar Hill. It is a truly calming space.

IF ONE THING COULD BE DEMOLISHED IT WOULD BE
There are a few particular buildings I can think of, but let me be diplomatic and keep it more general. I would be happy to take down any skyscraper or tall building in a heritage precinct.

MY CHOICE OF TRANSPORTATION
The local trains and buses. The bus company, *BEST*, is one of the largest in the world. They have a fleet of almost 5,000 buses plying more than 350 routes. They are crucial too in providing a West/East/West corridor, as trains or metros do not cover this yet.

WHAT WE CAN LEARN FROM MUMBAI
To me a city is a place where if you live in it, it helps you decide what you want to become. It will expose you to variety, diversity, and multiple of options and choices. Mumbai is that kind of a place. It allows you to learn from and about so many different options and opportunities.

INSTILLING A PASSION FOR ARCHITECTURE

ABHIJIT MANDREKAR

Abhijit Mandrekar (1961) earned a Bachelor's degree in Architecture from University of Bombay in India, and a Master's degree from the TU Delft in the Netherlands.

After graduation he worked on a broad variety of projects in Africa, the Netherlands and India. Since 1998, he has been running his own firm, *ArchSpace-M*. He has completed large-scale urban and regional planning projects as well as landscape, housing, industrial architecture and interior design assignments.

Between 1995 and 2003, in addition to his work as an architect, planner, landscape architect and interior designer, Abhijit also filled several teaching positions, among others at the TU Delft, the University of Mumbai and the University of Nairobi in Kenya.

Since 2010 Abhijit has divided his time between India and the Netherlands. He opened a second office of *ArchSpace-M* in Mumbai and works as a visiting professor at the IES College of Architecture and at the Academy of Architecture, both located in Mumbai.

We sit in the staff room on the fourth floor of IES College of Architecture in Bandra. Outside cars honk, above our heads fans whiz, and next to us faculty members discuss a town plan. They prevent the drawing from flying off the table by holding it by all four corners. In the study halls next door students work quietly on their projects. Meanwhile, over *dosa* and *chai*, we talk with architect and guest professor Abhijit Mandrekar, who, after spending twenty years in the Netherlands, recently returned to the city where he was born and brought up, to teach and to practise architecture.

SEPARATED BUT INSEPARABLE

'I want to use my experience as a professor and as an architect and urban planner to improve architectural education in Mumbai', Abhijit explains, when we ask him what made him take up the position at the college. 'The practice of architecture and architectural education should be strictly separated. Yet, the two should constantly feed each other, and are in essence inseparable.' And thus Abhijit urges his students in Mumbai to look beyond the walls of their college. He insists that they go to libraries and search the internet for new information. He encourages them to expand their horizons by attending seminars and conferences and most of all: by practising architecture, even while still in school. Just like he did during his studies in Mumbai. 'By stimulating the students in this way', he says, 'I hope to achieve something that at present merely seems to be some idealistic dream: I want the students here to develop a passion for architecture.'

INDIAN STUDENTS & DUTCH STUDENTS

Although Abhijit believes that the best students in India can measure themselves against the best students in the Netherlands, he does feel a little frustrated working in the Indian context. 'Students' effort is so minimal, that it is almost frustrating. Students in higher classes hardly ever attend the lectures, let alone produce work. In that sense TU Delft, where I used to teach, offers a more interesting experience.'

'Of course, students in Mumbai face difficulties that students in the Netherlands do not face', Abhijit admits. 'Being located in a rich country, TU Delft has many facilities. In Mumbai, the access to these facilities directly depends upon the financial condition and personal network of your parents. The yearly enrolment fee of this college is about INR 70,000. A lot of students with a genuine interest in architecture end up studying something else, because they can't afford the fees, or because another course seems to be a better investment', according to Abhijit.

But even after securing admission, a student's economic background still plays a vital role. Abhijit: 'Some students can afford more expensive materials for their projects than others. Architecture is an expensive course.'

PASSION FROM WITHIN

The education system itself also has an impact on the possibilities for students to excel, Abhijit feels. 'In Delft, the general level of work is fairly high. The system offers a possibility for weaker students to climb up to a certain level, but at the same time the very talented ones are brought down to the same standard.' The education system works as a leveller. 'When you graduate from Delft you are a good architect or perhaps even a very good architect, but never an exceptional one. Here in India, on the other hand, it is more a survival of the fittest. Students who are poor in their performance will not receive any extra attention or encouragement. But, those who are talented can attain great heights.'

The greatest difference of all, however, Abhijit thinks, is that in the Netherlands everyone who studies architecture actually wants to become an architect. 'They have a passion for the subject that comes from within. That passion automatically leads to better work. In India, many architecture students will end up doing something completely different. Or, when it comes to female students, they might never practise at all.'

FORM & FUNCTION

One of the things Abhijit was surprised to find was that the education system had not changed at all in his absence. 'The content of the courses is exactly the same as when I studied here. There is still a major focus on programme-oriented design.' Contextual approaches are left unexplored. 'This generation is what I call a three-screen generation', Abhijit says. 'The mobile phone screen, the computer screen and the TV screen: this generation finds these virtual worlds more interesting than reality. It is as if they feel that reality is nothing but a necessary ingredient that they need to live with, but given the opportunity they'd rather retreat into their trusted domain of virtual reality. For an architect that is problematic. Your building designs, drawings, and all other building-related issues can be developed on a computer, but the translations of it to reality have to be made.'

'Yet the curriculum follows a programmatic design approach', says Abhijit. 'Teachers and students alike seem to be so driven with programmatic distribution and programme related spaces... they do not seem to realize that a building can house a completely different programme in time and could and should be flexible! For example, today ancient structures such as monasteries are used as libraries, and temples as restaurants. The "form follows function" principle is not justified anymore.'

Designing in a context is something Abhijit himself learned abroad: first in Kenya, where he worked for almost four years, and after that in the Netherlands. 'Designing in a broader context is as challenging as making a great object. In Delft students learn in their first year how to "anchor" their architecture in a social, urban and even in a regional context, in many different ways. I would love to introduce that here as well. Unfortunately, here, as it is anywhere in the world, change is usually met with resistance and must be introduced gradually.'

EDUCATION AS BUSINESS

This resistance does not come from fellow faculty members, but comes from 'higher authorities', Abhijit experienced. 'The lack of change in the curriculum is a direct result of the way the education system is organized', he thinks. 'Colleges in Mumbai are affiliated to the universities. And these universities are not autonomous: a body of government officials directs them. The people in charge of developing and approving the curriculum are not necessarily architects. They are managers at best, politicians at worst. In any case, they may or may not have knowledge of architecture. Sure, an advisory panel with representatives of the faculty of the affiliated colleges gets to voice its opinions, but they may not have enough influence to bring about the necessary change.'

The decision-makers may not have the quality of education as their topmost priority. 'The primary concern of the Managing Heads is how to generate funds', Abhijit says. 'In a nutshell, it is all about the profits and it is a complex diplomatic, political game.'

ARCHITECTURE AS BUSINESS

Money matters not just in the field of architectural education, but also in architectural practice. 'The main concern of architects in Mumbai is: "How can I generate more money?"', says Abhijit. 'All architects here try to find loopholes in the rules and regulations commonly known as the Development Control Rules.' These rules govern the building activity in the city of Mumbai. Students learn about these rules during their fourth year in college. 'But', says Abhijit, 'they don't learn how to work around them'. He argues that in order to operate in Mumbai successfully it is imperative that you are aware of the invisible money streams. 'As soon as students step outside of the college they encounter these at all levels. For example, it is impossible to get approvals for your plans through normal, official procedures. Yet, the budgets, the financial frameworks and the hidden sources are never discussed in the lecture hall.'

LACK OF SPACE, MONEY, AND TRUST

What do Dutch architects need to learn when they come to Mumbai, we wonder. Abhijit is clear about this: they need to learn to work with the space and budget crunch. In his own career he had to unlearn this. 'My first assignment abroad was to design a restaurant. I remember myself working hard to use every square centimetre. That's what I was used to in my Mumbai practice. In Kenya, where I was at the time, they looked at my design and wondered why I focused so much on that. I had to change my thinking. It wasn't all about money and the space crunch anymore, as it was in Mumbai.'

'Secondly', Abhijit continues, 'those who want to succeed here need to realize that contracts have less or no value here.' 'A verbal agreement in India', he warns, 'is not equal to a written agreement, as it is in the Netherlands. In fact, a written agreement is not equal to a written agreement either.' He laughs when he says this. But then adds in a serious tone: 'A client here finds it absolutely normal to pay you less than what you had agreed upon. In fact, this, they think, is doing good business! And there is nothing you can do about this. Oh sure, go, take the client to court. But do you really want to do that, knowing that the case will run for the next ten or twenty years?'

He advises the Dutch who come to work in Mumbai to think more business-like. To trust people less than they do at home. 'The client might not mean what he says. He may say it only to make you feel good. Learn to operate with distrust and with no expectations. That's a tough one, but it's necessary if you want to succeed here.' He applies this principle to his own operations. 'I never do any work here without getting an advance payment. I would rather not work, than work without getting paid.'

INDIAN DESIGN

What Abhijit enjoys most now that he is back at work in Mumbai as an architect, is the design freedom it gives him. No one expects him to specialize. He can do urban planning, architecture, interior design and product design. And perhaps also take up his other interests, such as art direction and filmmaking. 'This multi-tasking would be impossible in the Netherlands', he thinks.

But he also likes working in Mumbai because he gets to design for a different climate. 'In the Netherlands a building, ultimately, is always an envelope', Abhijit says. 'The skin of the building separates the inside and the outside. The two worlds are completely separated no matter how thin and transparent the division between them may be. The Netherlands may have a technological advantage over India, but India has a design advantage over the Netherlands.' And then, philosophically, he adds, 'This is the age-old symbiosis between the East and the West: the West has the material advantage and the East, the spiritual advantage. Western Science and Eastern Wisdom. Both are essential to keep the balance in the world.'

LEARNING FROM...

Despite his criticism of the education, the attitude of students, and the way the business practice works in the city, Abhijit feels that there is enough the rest of the world can learn from Mumbai. The design freedom mentioned before is something he cherishes. But also the attitude of Indian architects, and Indians in general: 'I think Indians have a gift to work within extremely complex societal structures, are admirably flexible, and have a great tolerance for diversity. That's something the Dutch can surely learn from them.'

Abhijit explains that this is due to the type of society Indians grow up in. 'Indian society is extremely complex and diversity is its definition. People quickly learn to see through complexity, to work within it, and to remain flexible and tolerant.' This affects the architectural practice too. 'In the Netherlands you go to the municipal office, submit your paperwork, collect an approval stamp and you are through. In India you need to work within, in-between, through, and around written and unwritten rules.' He compares it with an onion. 'The bureaucratic process has many layers, where the next layer only becomes visible after having peeled off the previous one. And then, finally, and surprisingly, you discover that there is no centre.'

He does not want to say that the system in India or in the Netherlands is better per se, but rather that India, maybe inadvertently, teaches those who choose to operate within its system incredibly valuable skills that they can use to their advantage anywhere in the world: comprehending complex processes, being flexible and understanding diversity.

CHOWPATTY BEACH

MY MUMBAI
ABHIJIT MANDREKAR

MUMBAI IS SPECIAL BECAUSE
The city is special because of its multi-level complexity. There are so many contrasts and paradoxes. You see them in religion, caste, economic status, social interactions, costumes, ethnic differences, education levels, cuisines, hygienic and living conditions, transport methods, civic behaviours, work conditions, physical strength... etcetera, etcetera. The list is almost endless!

THIS CAN BE IMPROVED
I would like to see less corruption in the city.

MY FAVOURITE PLACE
Chowpatty Beach, located in the area called Girgaum, at the northern end of Marine Drive. It is one of the most popular and well-known beaches of Mumbai. Especially during *Ganesh Chaturthi*, the festival honouring the Hindu god Ganesh, the beach is packed with people. They come to immerse their idols of the god in the sea. The rest of the year it is a fabulous place to taste typical Indian snacks, such as *kulfi* [Indian ice cream] and *pani puri*.

MY FAVOURITE RESTAURANT
Samovar Café. It is located inside the *Jehangir Art Gallery* in Fort and overlooks the gardens of the *Prince of Wales Museum* [now called *Chhatrapati Shivaji Maharaj Vastu Sangahalaya*]. It is a perfect spot to relax and ponder over life in the city.

MY FAVOURITE LANDMARK
The *Gateway of India*. It is a monument in South Mumbai, a 25-metre high arch. The structure was built to commemorate the arrival of King George and Queen Mary in 1911. It was built on the place where passenger ships would arrive. The idea was that it would be the first structure for visitors to see and a grand welcome to the British rulers. But as it was completed only in 1924, George and Mary themselves saw only was the foundation stone and a model upon arrival. Although the structure in one way marks the peak of the British rule in India, it also symbolizes the end of it, as the last British troops left the country through the *Gateway* in 1948.

THE BEST PLACE TO RELAX
Inside one's own mind.

IF ONE THING COULD BE DEMOLISHED IT WOULD BE
The unreliable attitude of people.

MY CHOICE OF TRANSPORTATION
The local trains.

MY FAVOURITE MUMBAI FILM
There are so many films made in Mumbai and about Mumbai; in fact most films I saw in my childhood would somehow have an aspect of Mumbai in it. They show the beautiful and the ugly sides of the city. But no matter how beautiful or complete a movie may seem it is impossible to show all aspects of the city. *Slumdog Millionaire* (2008) is a film I would recommend. It made the different and secret worlds within Mumbai visible and accessible to each and everyone. And *Bombay* (1995), directed by Mani Ratnam, is worth watching as well. It centres on the tensions and violence between religious communities in 1992 and 1993.

WHAT WE CAN LEARN FROM MUMBAI
How we can cope with social, cultural and economic differences and complexities. How we can build up patience and translate it into relentless perseverance and turn it an advantage. How we can master skills to accept and understand surprises – both pleasant and unpleasant – and diversity.

THE NEXT GENERATION

MUMBAI'S YOUNG ARCHITECTS: SALONI DEODHAR, KARTIK GALA, SAPNA LAKHE AND SHWETAMBARI SHINDE

Saloni Deodhar (1986) gained her Bachelor's degree in Architecture at KRVIA in Mumbai in 2010. She joined *Deodhar Associates* the same year. Thanks to an exchange programme she gained international experience as a student at Bern University of Applied Sciences in Switzerland. She extended her stay abroad for seven months by taking up a position as intern (*praktikant*) in Bern with architecture and urban planning firm *Itten+Brechbühl.*

Kartik Gala (1985) completed his Bachelor's degree in Architecture at KRVIA in Mumbai in 2010. Upon graduation he did various interior design and landscape projects and joined his alma mater as Visiting Faculty, teaching Design Graphics, Computer Graphics and Landscape Design. Currently he is pursuing a Master's degree in Advanced Architecture from the Institute of Advanced Architecture of Catalonia in Barcelona, Spain.

Sapna Lakhe (1987) graduated in 2010 from KRVIA in Mumbai with a Bachelor's degree in Architecture. She then continued her studies at the Pratt Institute in New York in the USA, where she completed an MSc in Architecture and Urban Design in 2012. At present she is affiliated to the Balwant Sheth School of Architecture in Mumbai as Design Faculty and works as an architect and partner at *Sankraman Design Studio*, also in Mumbai.

Shwetambari Shinde (1986) obtained a Bachelor of Architecture degree from KRVIA in Mumbai in 2010. She followed up her studies with a course on Environment and Sustainable Development at the Center for Environmental Planning and Technology University (CEPT) in Ahmedabad. She worked as an architect with various firms in Mumbai, including *Deodhar Associates*. Currently she is an architect and partner at *Sankraman Design Studio* in Mumbai.

On a rainy afternoon, four young architects based in Mumbai gathered to talk about the present and the future of architecture in Mumbai. We wanted to meet because we wondered how the next generation of architects sees the architecture practice. What are, to them, the most important issues facing architects working in the city right now? What differences would they highlight between the Indian firms and the foreign firms they have worked for? And finally, we were curious to know what our interaction with them would teach us about practising architecture in general: What could we learn from these young Mumbai architects?

MUMBAI AS AN ARCHITECTURE HUB

All four young architects studied in Mumbai. They were classmates at the Kamla Raheja Vidyanidhi Institute for Architecture and Environmental Studies. The institute is relatively young: it was founded only in 1992. Yet, over the years it quickly built a solid reputation for itself as one of the premier schools of architecture in India. The courses at the institute are run under the aegis of the University of Mumbai. After shorter or longer stints abroad, all four young architects decided to work as architects in Mumbai. Why did they choose this city to work in, we first want to know. Sapna takes the lead and explains: 'It is a simple choice. Most of India's architecture firms are located in the city of Mumbai. Thus the infrastructure for young architects is best developed here.' Shwetambari adds, 'It also makes business sense for architecture firms to choose Mumbai as a base: there is cheap labour available, and it is the city where the headquarters of almost all the major corporate clients have a presence.' As a result, Mumbai has become India's architecture hub and a logical choice for young architects to start their career.

DEVELOPMENT MEANS REDEVELOPMENT

Working on projects in Mumbai often means working on redevelopment projects. The young architects express their concern over the consequences of the current lack of democracy in the design and building processes for slum areas and old residential neighbourhoods, where nowadays many rehabilitation and redevelopment projects take place. They feel that ideas and plans developed behind drawing tables and in conference rooms often do not fit the end-users. Kartik: 'New buildings in Mumbai are thought up by developers, not by architects or the communities who will use them. There is so much history in this city and there are so many distinct areas. But what happens now is that all this is making way for uniformity. The *gaothans* [old village sites] with their distinct *wadis* [lanes] and other particular features, like their different colour schemes and elaborate facades, are being demolished. And what happens next? We, the architects and developers, often impose our ideas. We try to make the area look like something else. We try to make it something we thought of without looking at the people who will use it. And you can guess what will happen... We see a clash, as the end-users use the design differently than we intended them to do.'

CLASHES

The young architects emphasize that this is not the story of one particular neighbourhood in Mumbai, but very much the story of Mumbai as a whole. In fact, at present the entire east side of the city – roughly speaking, the areas adjacent to the Central and Harbour [railway] Lines – is now being considered for redevelopment. About forty percent of the population of the city lives in this area.

The type of 'clashes' between the ideas of developers and architects and the wishes of the end-users vary. Kartik gives a concrete example of how architecture for slum rehabilitation should incorporate the ideas of functionality alive among the slum dwellers themselves. 'Take Dharavi [Mumbai's largest slum]', he begins. 'We know that if you put up buildings with only retail shops at the bottom it is not going to be a successful project. It is simply not going to work as people have sweatshops over there. And they live above those manufacturing units, those small factories. Due to the ways we build houses for them, we now actually force them to change the way they live...'

Yet, despite this awareness of regular mismatches between design and functionality, and despite the good intentions, we also find that some of the problems slum rehabilitation projects face, such as bad construction, bad maintenance etc., are rather easily blamed on the alleged attitude of the slum dwellers, and not taken up as a design challenge for the architect, or an issue for the builder. Says Saloni: 'You know with these projects that after two years the buildings will be completely messed up. (...) So what we [architects] imagine and want to give them [the slum dwellers] is never reached to that level.'

RULES AND REGULATIONS

Other features of the architectural present in Mumbai that recur throughout the discussion are the lack of planning and the uniformity of the buildings constructed in the past decades. The young architects see two major culprits: the pace at which the city was growing, which means that there is 'simply no time for planning', on the one hand, and the extensive number of rules and regulations on the other. Because of these two factors, the architects argue 'you simply keep making the same type of buildings'. They do have ideas on how this situation could be improved. There should be more time to plan, and fewer – or at least different – rules, so that architects have more freedom to design. In addition, 'a body of architects should be set up that can step in to give counterweight to the bureaucratic factor, which at present is always the dominating factor'. However, that Mumbai's architecture will always come about in a highly regulated environment nevertheless seems a given to them. The space crunch, invoked by the city's high population density, and its location on an island, simply make an elaborate rulebook a necessity. 'In New Delhi there is less need for extensive regulation. There is more space. And as a result projects can be more lavish', Kartik feels.

EAST MEETS WEST

The young architects display a critical attitude towards Western architecture based on the realization that the West and India represent different contexts with different demands. Sapna expresses this sentiment as follows: 'A lot of the developments in India are very much based on Western influences. But why should we follow these, while the people there are actually trying to reinvent what they are doing? What happens here is that we are falling in the same trap as they, in the West, did before us. What this trap is? The crazy developments we see all around us here! We should take a step back and ask ourselves first: What is the right way to develop?'

Their critical attitude is also based on their own experiences. Frustration with the lack of democracy in the design process raised the expectation among some of the young architects that they would experience a more democratic design culture at foreign architecture firms; they were to find, however, that they had been naive. Granted, some did find the desired design atmosphere, particularly those working in smaller firms and on smaller projects. But as Saloni explains, this was not necessarily the case. 'I found, while working in Switzerland, that the government was involved in most projects we did. I think this was the main reason for the lack of direct engagement of communities involved. The bureaucratic planning factor outweighed other voices. Further, a lot of the projects were competition projects and not live ones. That restricted and prevented to a great extent the interaction and focus on the end-users. So no, I found that it was not necessarily a more democratic affair there than the way it is done here in Mumbai.'

Furthermore, at Western firms some of the architects were surprised to find a heavy emphasis on the technical aspects of architectural work practice, and in particular on details. 'The way of working at the European firm I was employed at was very technically oriented. It was a mass production firm. I felt they got out of architecture as soon as possible and after that only focused on the details. To be frank, I sometimes felt like being in a machine', Sapna recalls.

ACTIVISM

The young architects try their best to not become discouraged by all the factors that make imaginative and creative architecture so difficult to make and sell in Mumbai: the rules and regulations, the importance of having and maintaining a powerful network, the incredibly fast pace of development in their city, the space constraints, the absence of a competition culture and the power of developers over architects. Most of them seem to have quickly learned how to operate in Mumbai's current architecture practice, how to navigate the many pitfalls these factors lead to on a daily basis. The dissatisfaction, however, lingers. They feel certain questions need to be asked by their own generation of architects, particularly with regard to identity: Where can we find the Indian identity? How can we maintain the good qualities of 'the old' when designing something 'new'? How can we design in such a way that it fits the actual Indian end-users best?

To keep engaging with these – and other – questions, they started a discussion forum. They called it *Beehive*. Although it is still in its very early stages, they intend it to become a lively platform for 'young architects who want to give something back to the city'. So far they have set out to collectively make designs and have submitted one of those for a competition in Stuttgart, Germany. In addition, they hold brainstorm sessions together. This way they expose themselves to each other's and to foreign ideas and force each other to think about their own particular environment.

CHARLES CORREA

Interestingly, India's most famed architect, Charles Correa, who concerned himself with the same set of questions, is not seen as an example. When we ask whether they feel his architecture to be 'truly Indian', their reactions show that although they admire his incorporation of old and new Indian ideas, they are critical of the success of his designs. 'The concepts he uses are Indian, in the sense that he really looks at the way people live', Kartik says. 'For example, he carefully studies the kind of requirements they need to be able to live in India's [hot] climate and how they live together as communities, rather than as single units. These things are very well incorporated in his work. It is what makes his work "Indian". You can see that in his work for Navi Mumbai. There, housing is built around courtyards, providing families with some individual space, while simultaneously staying connected to others. That structure of building, and the idea to build in a grid pattern, goes all the way back to how ancient Indians built at Harappa [the ancient city of the Indus Valley Civilization, that emerged around 2600 BC]. But we don't see Correa's work as very successful. Navi Mumbai works because people need it. There is no other place to go. He applied the same ideas in Chandigarh and we consider that a failure. It never developed its own identity as a city.'

LEARNING FROM...

Although they are searching for many answers themselves, Mumbai's young architects can already teach us a variety of things. For example, how to work *within* the rules and *with* the rules. We can learn from their experiences which rules may provide an incentive for better design, and which regulations could hamper creativity. They are also in the position to share what too much and too little government involvement entails. Their experiences further force us to reconsider to what extent our focus on details is justified. Does it stand in the way of our core assignment as architects?

Finally, some of their discourse, unintentionally, suggests that for Mumbai's slum redevelopment to really become something more than 'fitting a maximum number of people in a minimum amount of space', the awareness that end-users may have different wishes than developers and architects is but a beginning. An important beginning, but maybe not be enough to make these projects sustainable.

DN ROAD, FORT

MY MUMBAI

SAPNA LAKHE

MUMBAI IS SPECIAL BECAUSE

Mumbai is one of those cities that has moulded, shaped and reshaped itself over time to accommodate every kind of person.

MY FAVOURITE PLACE

I have lived in South Mumbai most of my life and *Colaba* is one of my favourite places to be. I like its multicultural appeal, the exotic European and Lebanese food, and the traditional and rare items you can find in the street market. It is definitely worth the walk on a crowded sidewalk.

MY FAVOURITE RESTAURANT

The Tea Centre, near Churchgate Railway Station is very old, but not too well known. Even though it is not located in a very exciting building, I love its colonial ambiance inside and that they have varieties of tea from all over the world.

MY FAVOURITE LANDMARK

The *Chhatrapati Shivaji Terminus* [formerly known as Victoria Terminus] is one of the finest landmarks that the city has. The grandeur and the expert engineering of this railway station make it one of my favourite landmarks in the city. It was built between 1878 and 1887 to commemorate the Golden Jubilee of Queen Victoria and is now a UNESCO World Heritage site. It mixes Gothic Revival architecture with traditional Indian styles.

THE BEST PLACE TO RELAX

The promenades along Mumbai's coastline, such as Marine Drive, the Worli Seaface, Bandra Bandstand and Carter Rd. in Bandra. They take you away from the city, while still being a part of it.

IF ONE THING COULD BE DEMOLISHED IT WOULD BE

Recently, there has been a huge debate over the list of heritage structures [a percentage of it being residential buildings] in Mumbai. For some occupants and owners of these houses, their buildings being listed as heritage structures has become a problem. They suddenly face huge maintenance costs, and I think it is necessary to be sensitive towards the owners. Some of these structures should be considered for demolition, and others renovated with external funds.

MY CHOICE OF TRANSPORTATION

The local trains are the most definite choice of transportation in the city. The trains carry millions every day.

MY FAVOURITE MUMBAI BOOK

Bombay. The Cities Within (1995). It is a book compiled by Sharada Dwivedi and Rahul Mehrotra. The book covers the history of the seven islands that now make up Mumbai and has lots of old photographs, paintings and sketches. It gives a good insight into the fabric of the city.

MY FAVOURITE MUMBAI FILM

Seven Islands and a Metro, a 2006 documentary by Madhushree Dutta. It captures in particular the deep-rooted multiculturalism of the city.

WHAT WE CAN LEARN FROM MUMBAI

Being someone who migrated to this city from a smaller town in Maharashtra state, I learned to adapt and adjust to the restrictive environments of the city. This city has much less than a square metre of open space for each of its residents. So you learn to make the most of the space available.

FROM THE NETHERLANDS TO INDIA… AND BEYOND

SHYAM KHANDEKAR

Shyam Khandekar (1951) completed a Bachelor's degree in Architecture (with honours) at the IIT in Kharagpur, India. He subsequently obtained an MSc in Urban Planning from the TU Delft in the Netherlands, and an MA in Urban Design from the University of Manchester in the United Kingdom.

He worked at various architecture and design firms in India and Europe, before starting his own practice *Khandekar: Urban Design and Landscape* in 1988 in the Netherlands. In 2008 his firm merged with *BDP*, to become *BDP Khandekar*. He is currently a member of the Board of Directors of *BDP International*, and Chairman of *BDP*'s Dutch and Indian studios. His expertise as an architect is combining essential aspects of urban design, landscape architecture and infrastructure in projects. He has also lectured extensively on liveable cities.

Shyam has won international awards with two of his housing and urban regeneration projects in the Netherlands (i.e. Monnikenhuizen in Arnhem and Paleiskwartier in Den Bosch) and received wide acclaim for his plans for regenerating the historic town of Coevorden. *Nirlon Knowledge Park*, his first Indian project, won the *International Property Award 2012* – Asia Pacific Region. Presently he is leading the design team for a sustainable new IIT campus in Jodhpur, India.

'I was not interested to work in China since I could not design for a society I did not know or understand. I had no idea how to operate there. India I knew. And now, returning to India, I can build on twenty-five years of experience and knowledge accumulated in the Netherlands. I return to India in maturity.'

FIRST STEPS IN INDIA

Although born and brought up in India, Shyam Khandekar's professional association with the country goes back only six years. 'In 2006 we were approached by an entrepreneur from New Delhi to design what he called a knowledge park for him. This was at the time when the real estate boom had just started', Shyam says. 'As these things often go, this project did not materialize, but we did get to know another consultant. And later we learned that he had talked about us to other potential clients.'

And so it happened that one day, back in his office in the Netherlands, Shyam received a phone call from Mumbai. 'The man on the other end of the line told me: "We have 25 acres to develop in the heart of Mumbai. We have set up an international competition. Two foreign firms and two Indian firms have started their work on it. I heard your name, I heard you are Indian, but settled abroad, and I think you would be an interesting addition to the competition."'

The caller was Kunal Sagar, the Executive Vice Chairman and grandson of the founder of *Nirlon Ltd*, a firm that manufactured nylon yarn. *Nirlon* had shifted its manufacturing out of Mumbai, and wanted to redevelop the plot where the factory used to be. Shyam negotiated the terms and conditions, and accepted the offer to participate in the competition. He went on to not just win the assignment, but to win several national and international awards with his design for the *Nirlon Knowledge Park*.

WINNING TRUST

Gaining a client's trust is a key factor in developing business in India, Shyam thinks. 'You have to invest and you have to be lucky that you meet the right person.' For Shyam, trust-building with his first Indian client started right from the first phone call. 'When they asked me to participate in their competition they put down several conditions. One of these was that they wanted me to personally visit the site in Mumbai and then to visit it again within three weeks to discuss the initial concept. I did visit the site to understand it, but requested the client to visit me in the Netherlands three weeks later.' The client agreed. And when he came to the Netherlands, Shyam took time off to show the potential client some of his other projects and introduced him to several previous clients.

'After our discussions on Saturday, I had been working on the sketches that night. I had a few questions still and felt I had to clarify those before Kunal [Sagar] would step on the plane. I decided to call him... on a Sunday morning at 9 a.m. Later Kunal told me he was impressed I was willing to work on Saturdays and Sundays. He had experienced that was very uncommon among Westerners, and he felt it showed I'm passionate about my work. My phone call on Sunday morning, he told me later, assured him that "my heart was in it".'

This commitment was not what made Shyam win the competition. 'The client said it was our design that made us win, but I think it surely helped to build a relation of trust between the two of us', Shyam says, adding with a smile, 'It lay the foundations for a very durable and pleasant working relationship – a fruitful relationship which has now lasted for six years with a promise of many years to come!'

NIRLON KNOWLEDGE PARK

Shyam and his team in the Netherlands designed an office park of about ten hectares (25 acres) where 20,000 people would work. 'It came with a lot of freedom', Shyam recalls. 'The only thing that was determined in the zoning plan was that we should build an office park and that it should have an FSI of maximum 2.0. Otherwise we were free to do as we liked. That was quite a change from what we were used to in the Netherlands. There, a far more detailed vision is generally embedded in the zoning plan and you have to make your plans and designs with that in mind.'

Outlining his vision behind the master plan and landscaping, Shyam says: 'The starting premise of our design was that we wanted to create an office park with a unique identity – a green oasis in a chaotic and bustling city where more than 20,000 users would work with pleasure. All the people who are to work in these offices need an outside space, we felt. We want cars to leave the terrain quickly and not intervene with pedestrians. What we did was design the entire plan around a grand central park. We connected all the buildings to roads on the outside. And from the inside the buildings face the park.'

An interesting feature is that some of the old industrial structures have been preserved. The cooling tower, for example, received a prominent position in the plan, as a central hub where cafés would be situated. Initially the client was not interested in maintaining old buildings. 'They were in fact amused when we suggested it', Shyam recalls. 'But now they are quite happy that some of the rich history of *Nirlon* has been retained, and gives the *Knowledge Park* a unique identity.'

EFFICIENT MEETINGS

One thing Shyam is visibly impressed with is the speed with which the master plan for *Nirlon* was designed and adopted. 'It was hectic', Shyam recalls, 'as real estate prices went up. Each delay literally cost money. So together with one of my designers I flew to India every two weeks. We only needed three sessions to establish the essentials of the master plan. In the meantime we helped decide on the basic structure of the buildings.'

The way the meetings were conducted provides the explanation for the work tempo and efficiency. Shyam shares: 'In the Netherlands a meeting means you give each other the information you have, you go home to find solutions, and reconvene. But the structure and goal of meetings at *Nirlon* was different. During one of my first visits to India for the *Nirlon* project, I found myself in a room with a long table. Around it were about twelve persons, all specialists: an air conditioning specialist, a parking expert, a man who knew everything about facade materials, a financial man, etc. Behind them sat their assistants, about three or four each. In the morning every expert in the meeting made a short presentation in which they shared basic information. After that, everyone, including even the real estate agent, voiced his or her opinion about the solutions presented. For example, when we talked about the cooling system to be used in the buildings, the man in charge of the rentals would bring up that the tenants would not appreciate a specific type of system. The sustainability expert gave his point of view in the light of the certification he aimed for. The financial guy would argue for or against the idea based on his budget calculations; and I, as the chief designer, put my worries on the table regarding the space a system like that would take.'

The morning session concluded, the assistants were sent out to find answers to the questions that came up in the morning. 'In the late afternoon, they would rejoin the meeting to share the answers they collected with the core team and the client.' And most remarkable of all: 'The client, in the person of Kunal Sagar, would the very same day take the necessary decisions. This was not only very brave, but required remarkable insight!'

Shyam thinks this model worked so well because the client was committed and had decision-making powers. But he warns that this type of chain integration is not the norm yet in India – but in fact the exception. 'Whether or not you can work efficiently in India, depends very much on whether the client is willing to invest his personal time in the process. And if he is on top of it and himself takes part in the process then one can work really fast.' Faster than in the Netherlands with its consensus model.

MERGING WITH BDP

A year after the start of Nirlon, Shyam started looking around for new projects in India for his Dutch studio *Khandekar: Urban Design and Landscape*. Some worked out and some didn't, but steadily his portfolio in the region grew.

Soon he was approached by *BDP*, Europe's largest design firm, with a staff of 1300. 'They had about twenty company directors and asked me to become one of them and to bring my Dutch practice into theirs. I took the offer. For me it meant that, after twenty-five years of working in the Netherlands, I got a new challenge and the opportunity to operate more internationally.'

INDIAN ENGLISH

Working together with *BDP* had some very practical advantages for the Dutch practice of *Khandekar: Urban Design and Landscape*. 'Working from the Netherlands we had one real handicap', Shyam explains. 'The Dutch can speak English well enough to buy a kilo of tomatoes, but to have technical discussions in English over the phone is a different matter, especially when both sides struggle understanding each other's accents. You can have a fabulous landscaper in your firm, but he is useless if he is unable to communicate with the client. So either I, or my co-director Liesl Vivier, who comes from South Africa, had to intervene and help with the communication. This limited our potential to work in India. Cooperating with *BDP*, an English firm, meant we suddenly had people who understood and could communicate much better in [Indian] English. In this way the merger had an unexpected benefit for us.'

DELHI STUDIO

Not long after the merger of *Khandekar* with *BDP*, it became clear that with the increasing number of assignments in India the 'suitcase model' was no longer tenable. It was decided to set up a studio in New Delhi. Shyam was asked by the Board of Directors in London to become the Chairman of *BDP*'s and *Khandekar*'s joint operation in India. At present, about twenty-five creative professionals work at the multidisciplinary New Delhi studio.

Shyam points out one of the difficulties of setting up an office in India. 'It is the story of the chicken and the egg. When you meet clients they ask you where your team is. But you cannot build a team, unless you have projects to work on.'

When he found that he had been able to attract a few bright designers, but not enough projects to keep them occupied, Shyam decided to have them work on an academic project on a topic of great relevance to Indian cities, namely the walkability in urban areas in the context of the increasing use of cars. 'We took one of the DDA [Delhi Development Authority] colonies – residential complexes in Delhi that are forty years old – as a case study', Shyam explains. 'This colony consists of about six hundred apartments each, spread over buildings of some three-four stories high. We talked with the residents to find out what problems they were facing and learned that the high number of cars per colony was of one of them. In the original design there was space allocated for about 550 garages and fifty car parking spaces along roads, but at present the number of cars owned by the residents totalled about eighteen hundred! Each household had on average three cars. None of them is parked in the garage, and thus all these cars clutter the streetscape.'

The high number of cars per household was partially due to the fact that many apartments house joint families. But another reason, Shyam learned, was the taxation system. 'As you pay all your taxes at once when you purchase the car, it does not cost money to keep an unused car. Yet, it does cost money to have it removed...'

Shyam and his Delhi team did an intensive study of the traffic flows in the colonies and designed solutions for improvement. They presented their work at an Urban Mobility Conference in New Delhi, and were covered in several media. This gave *BDP Khandekar* publicity in India and, in turn, attracted new clients.

OTHER PROJECTS

In 2012 Shyam's Indian portfolio has grown exponentially. Work is either completed or underway at locations in Mumbai, Pune, Lonavla, Himachal Pradesh and Kerala. On top of that he is designing campuses for two IIT (Indian Institute of Technology) projects in regions that could not differ more in landscape and climate. The first is in Mandi, in the hilly state of Himachal Pradesh, the second in Jodhpur, in the desert state of Rajasthan. In both cases, Shyam emphasizes, the designs are not about what he likes, but what fits the environment best. 'In Mandi we should not want to build an icon of a building, but work with the hills. When we presented our design we told the clients: "No building can compete with these majestic hills. So what we do is make smaller structures located on terraces, that blend in with the landscape."'

In Jodhpur Shyam's concern is how he can protect the buildings from the harsh sunshine and make the most of occasional downpours. 'If there are rocks, we build our structures close to them, as the warm air flows over them. Further, we are going to build in such a way that the structures protect each other from the sun. And in our landscaping we aim to collect rainwater in low-lying areas, where evaporation is least.'

BHOPAL

In addition to travelling to India to work on projects, Shyam also lectures at the School of Planning and Architecture in Bhopal, the capital of the state of Madhya Pradesh, where he was born and brought up. The School is new, and is modelled after the institute of the same name in New Delhi. 'The aim of the central government is to make this SPA, and the four others that have been founded, "Institutes of Excellence"', Shyam explains.

'I am a Visiting Professor of the School, I teach at the Master's course in Urban Design.' His choice for Bhopal was a conscious one. 'I am from Madhya

Pradesh myself, and wanted to give something back.' But more importantly, Shyam feels that it is these smaller cities, which still host populations of several millions each, that are too often neglected in favour of Mumbai and New Delhi. 'If you really want to learn from India, I urge you to look beyond Mumbai and New Delhi', he says. 'Go to Pune, Gwalior, Jodhpur, and similar cities as well. I tell my students the same. When they select their projects I tell them to focus on these cities for a change. They make up a big part of what India is today.'

COMPUTER GENERATED IMAGES

What do you think Dutch architects must know when they want to start in India, we ask. 'You must know that Indian clients generally can't read drawings', Shyam says. 'What they really want you to make are computer generated images [CGI]. In the Netherlands we do that at a later stage, if we do it at all. First we sketch, then we make more detailed drawings, and then we might make a CGI version. But if you work in this sequence in India, you will find that six months into the project you have used up all of your fees, while the client thinks you have just started.' Shyam himself did not alter his mode of operation. 'I didn't use CGI, and I still don't. I make sketches, but knowing now what a client expects in each phase helps me to stay within budget and timelines.'

Another difference Shyam noticed was that Indian architects generally do not make a section drawing. 'They may occasionally make a model, but more often they only draw floor plans.'

BIGGER COMPANY, BIGGER RISKS

Shyam thinks that one of the reasons he has been successful in India is that he was relatively unknown. 'Big names from Europe are regularly invited to work in India, but they are more vulnerable to abuse. It happens often enough that a potential client calls them, pays for a concept, and then says, "Thank you, I have enough, I'll take it from here". Even though the final product may not be one the architect likes, the client will still market it using the name of the famous architect or firm.' Shyam compares it to being a beautiful woman, or a millionaire. 'When you are beautiful or rich you always have to wonder whether you are invited because of your looks or wealth, or because they really like you and appreciate your work.'

CONQUERING THE WORLD

The New Delhi studio is no longer just working on projects in India: there is an assignment in Nigeria, there are two ongoing projects in Bhutan, a building in Malaysia that was recently short-listed in a competition, and there are talks with a client in Mauritius. While showing us drawings and sketches of each of these projects, Shyam succinctly summarizes his main unexpected discovery upon branching out to India. 'India is centrally located. If you are an international firm, or if you want to be an international firm, one thing you should do is move part of your operations to a central location. That way, I found, you can also operate in surrounding countries.'

When he received the phone call from *Nirlon*, Shyam was 'still somewhat hesitating whether to start in India at all'. And he surely did not have the ambition to conquer the world. Yet, six years later, it is beginning to look like that is exactly what he is doing.

URBAN DESIGN AND LANDSCAPE ARCHITECTURE: BDP.KHANDEKAR

ARCHITECT: VENKATARAMANAN ASSOCIATES, BANGALORE

NIRLON KNOWLEDGE PARK, GOREGAON

NIRLON KNOWLEDGE PARK, GOREGAON

SV RD., BANDRA

MY MUMBAI
SHYAM KHANDEKAR

MY FAVOURITE PLACE
Juhu Beach. If you go there at three in the afternoon it is still quiet, as it is too hot. At around four or five o' clock the people start coming. What I like about it is that it attracts all kinds of people: rich and poor alike. Some come to play cricket, others for a jog, some for a snack, and again others for cocktails in one of the bars.

THIS CAN BE IMPROVED
The 'walkability' of the city. Freedom fighter Lokmanya Tilak (1856-1920) once said: 'Independence is our birthright'. I say: To be able to walk in a city is our birthright! Walking has so many benefits: it enhances equality, is good for health, for the environment, and has economic advantages as well.

MY FAVOURITE RESTAURANT
In Mumbai I love going to a restaurant that serves the traditional Indian *thali* [a set meal of various dishes served on a large plate]. There are a quite a few of these still around serving Gujarati, Marathi or Rajasthani food. Just wonderful!

MY FAVOURITE LANDMARK
Instead of a particular building, I like to think of water. So maybe Marine Drive? The water, the space, the curve... That is more Mumbai to me than any specific building adorning the promenade. The buildings will come and go in decades to come, but the space will remain.

THE BEST PLACE TO RELAX
Unpretentious Manori, just outside of Mumbai. It is a small peninsula, and reachable with a ferry from Marve beach. The boat carries the fisher folk mostly, who live there. The ferry ride takes only fifteen minutes. Just a stone's throw away from hectic Mumbai there is a paradise!

IF ONE THING COULD BE DEMOLISHED IT WOULD BE
Many of the newer buildings built in the building boom of the last years, in which the architect has not addressed the relationship of the building to the public realm, but only tried to maximize the built-up area for his client. Unfortunately more than half the buildings recently constructed in Mumbai will qualify.

MY CHOICE OF TRANSPORTATION
Cities are best appreciated and most liveable and sustainable if its residents can walk to their destinations. Children should be able to walk to their schools, the parents to their workplace and the older generation to their parks. We must learn to give preference to our pedestrians and cyclists in the city.

WHAT WE CAN LEARN FROM MUMBAI
Optimism. We have everything here in the Netherlands, but we do not realize it enough. I remember one time when I came back from India I had a newspaper with me. At Schiphol Airport I bought a Dutch newspaper and I compared the two. The mood in the Dutch paper was down. Yes, maybe economic growth has slowed down, but we are still at a level that India won't even reach in another thirty years...

ACTIVISM AND ARCHITECTURE

PK DAS

PK Das (1955) obtained his Bachelor's degree in Architecture from Sir J.J. College of Architecture in Mumbai. In 1980, not long after his graduation, he started his own practice: *PK Das & Associates*.

Already during his years as a student, he started collaborating with NGOs, community movements and self-help groups in pursuit of improving the lives of slum dwellers in the city. Ever since, he has been an active participant in the struggle for affordable housing models. At the same time he worked extensively on the reclaiming of public space, urban renewal and conservation. He is the Joint Convener of the housing rights organization called *Nivara Hakk Suraksha Samiti*, Chairperson of the *Mumbai Waterfronts Centre* and a member of the Steering Committee set up by the MMRDA (Mumbai Metropolitan Region Development Authority) for the preparation of a *Vision Plan 2050* for the Mumbai Metropolitan Region.

In addition to his activism and architectural work, which includes residential, institutional, commercial and landscaping projects, PK Das has delivered talks and lectures across the world. He is Adjunct Professor at the Department of Sociology of the University of Mumbai, and a visiting faculty member of KRVIA in Mumbai and the Centre for Environmental Planning and Technology (CEPT) in Ahmedabad.

It is late afternoon and we are standing in front of the window on the top floor of *PK Das & Associates'* office. While we watch lights being switched on in the buildings around us, the founder and director of the firm, PK Das, muses, 'We are like a watchtower in the neighbourhood. From here we have seen it happening: the disappearance of the [textile mill] worker colonies. The buildings and their people are all gone. All we see now from our windows are stereotypical towering walls. These five hundred acres in Central Mumbai could have altered the city. But it is too late now. It is all gone.'

ACTIVISM

Prabhadevi, the area in Central Mumbai that PK Das is talking about, is filled with up-market shops, restaurants and upper-middle class housing complexes with an average of some fifteen stories per building. The lower-middle class workers formerly residing there have shifted to other areas, as the provision of affordable housing was first reduced, and later mostly axed from the developers' plans. Yet, with almost sixty percent of Mumbai's population living in slums, and another significant percentage living in dilapidated apartment blocks, affordable housing remains a major issue. PK Das has worked and continues to work on slum rehabilitation projects. He sees this as a part of his activism as much as a part of his architecture. Activism and architecture, and particularly the combination of the two, is what defines him.

ADAPTATIONS

PK Das relates how other developers adapted his pioneering work in more humane designs for slum rehabilitation. It is not that he does not want them to copy his designs. He is too much of an activist to be bothered by this. His disappointment lays in the fact that his designs have been used superficially. The plan footprints were imitated, while the underlying ideas on spatial quality were thrown away. 'With our slum rehabilitation project in Chandivali we showed that we – architects and developers – can do much more than building unappealing rows of rectangular blocks', he explains. 'We showed another way of dealing with high density, by building around courtyards. These would not be towers [i.e. high-rise buildings]. The buildings go to the fourth floor only. Soon our plan spread like a wildfire among developers. They also started designing around courtyards, but they lost the scale and thereby displaced the idea totally.'

Instead of the four to seven stories PK Das designed, these other developers stacked up apartments up to twenty-three stories. And with that the same issues of the old way of building slum resettlements resurfaced: the bottom floors receive no natural light, nor fresh air, and the open spaces between blocks – the courtyards – become dark, cold, wasted areas, with no other use than indeed collecting waste. Housing for the poor thus had once again been 'reduced to a game of numbers', PK Das feels.

OPEN SPACES

Although he has strong opinions on what is lacking in Mumbai, and what is fantastic about it, he does not see himself as a 'creator of ideas'. 'The social movements develop the ideas', Das explains. 'I associate with them and translate their ideas into the best possible forms of spaces and structures. There are different stakeholders in any project and I, as an architect, am the bonding between them.' Nevertheless, he has also initiated several major projects – particularly in relation to the expansion and democratization of Mumbai's public open spaces.

In 1997 he started with a survey on Mumbai's waterfronts. The subsequent report documented the extent of coastline degradation and contained several plans and ideas to regenerate the same. In his 2011 publication *On The Waterfront. Reclaiming Mumbai's Open Spaces*, written in collaboration with sociologist Indra Munshi, PK Das explains his focus on these sites in particular. 'For millions who live in the crowded city, the waterfronts (...) are the only major open spaces apart from the few parks and maidans. (...) Despite their historical significance and importance as vital open spaces for a densely populated and highly congested city, waterfronts, particularly those in the suburbs, are facing degradation and have become the city's dumping grounds'[1]

CAUSES OF NEGLECT

A lack of attention and a lack of coordination between the different bodies that own the land have caused the sorry status of Mumbai's open spaces, PK Das thinks. Mumbai's Development Plans, which provide the official blueprint for the city's land use and development and are renewed every twenty years, either do not mention open spaces at all, or when they do, fail to provide a comprehensive guideline for their protection, conservation and enhancement.

In *On the Waterfront* PK Das explains the situation: 'Spaces in Mumbai are planned from the point of view of their value as real estate, so that public space is seen as the space left over after construction or development. We tend to look at reclamations, flyovers, highways, buildings – in short, all construction – as symbols of urban planning and progress. However it becomes increasingly clear that without long-term holistic planning these visible symbols of modernity do not necessarily enhance the quality of urban existence.'

BANDRA'S WATERFRONTS

After presenting the results of his 1997 survey at a public meeting in Bandra, PK Das invited NGOs, local residents' organizations, senior bureaucrats, and other concerned citizens to discuss the issue. During various meetings he outlined the problems and some of his solutions for the redevelopment of three waterfront areas: Bandra Bandstand, Bandra's Land's End, and Carter Rd. And he requested the participation of the various stakeholders and their input for the final plans.

The solutions he drew up for the regeneration of Bandra's waterfronts were simple, modest and practical. No major construction on the waterfronts was necessary, he felt. On the contrary, he presented a view 'to halt the abuse of the waterfronts and reallocate spaces and activities with minimum restructuring'. The underlying philosophy was that the waterfronts should remain 'the collective asset of the citizens and a vital vibrant element of the city's environmental and social fabric'.[2]

PROMENADES

On both Bandra Bandstand and Carter Road PK Das proposed building promenades: paved pathways along the coast with palm plantations, a children's park, a pet park and an amphitheatre. He maintained the natural contours of the waterfront. As the bureaucratic process took a long time, but residents were eager to see the plans realized, the work at Bandstand started before all the necessary approvals from the Municipal Corporation came in. A year later, in 2000, the promenade was officially inaugurated.

At Carter Road the Municipal Corporation had drafted its own regeneration plans, and even started work on these back in 1991. The residents opposed it, however, due to the shoreline being altered, and the mangroves damaged. So the work was stalled and went unfinished. Upon completion of the Bandstand project, PK Das stepped in. He encountered many bureaucratic obstacles, so much so that in *On The Waterfront* he and Munshi write: 'It would be too charitable to put this [the delays] down to conventional bureaucracy: in all probability, this intervention by citizens challenged the arrangements that officials from the BMC to the police maintain with regards to commissions on permissions, *haftas* from hawkers and other such illegal payments.'[3] Eventually the work was completed and a 1.3 kilometre-long promenade created. It was opened to public in 2002.

The same year he and the residents' association won a long battle with developers, government authorities, and private parties (in particular hotels) over the plot at Land's End – a significant heritage precinct. They set out to restore the dilapidated *Bandra Fort* located there and to make a garden. Thereby again adding a substantial amount of square metres to the open space available to the general public.

FUNDING FOR PROJECTS

PK Das shares that, in addition to obtaining permissions, generating funds is a major bottleneck for projects concerning public spaces. In the Bandra projects he found a committed collaborator and sponsor in actor and activist Shabana Azmi. As a Member of Parliament for the Rajya Sabha (India's House of Lords), she was allotted INR 10,000,000 under the Member of Parliament Local Area Development Scheme (MPLAD). More often than not these funds, allocated to each MP in India, go unused. Azmi, however, decided to use them to sponsor first the Bandstand plan, and later the Carter Road and Land's End projects.

Funds were also generated from private parties such as companies, but only on the strict condition that the contributions were routed through the citizens' association and the spaces thus created remained open for public use. The private sponsor entered into agreements with the local residents' associations, thereby ensuring collective control. 'This corporate sponsorship became more easy to obtain once a project was already underway and had received some press coverage', PK Das explains.

An important factor in the success of Bandra's seafront projects is the maintenance conducted *after* construction. For the Bandstand promenade the maintenance costs amount to approximately INR 30,000 per month. 'This is collected from some 150 buildings in the neighbourhood. The residents association that is responsible for the maintenance appeals to these buildings to contribute INR 20 per apartment per month. An added advantage of generating the necessary funds this way is it also promotes collective ownership of the public space', PK Das tells.

OPEN SPACES

The Bandra projects completed and several other projects underway, in 2011 PK Das gave his movement to create more open spaces in the city a new stimulus by mapping the entire city to find out how many open spaces Mumbai really has; information that was neither available from government authorities nor from private parties. He found that the available open space per 1,000 inhabitants was extremely low and declining. Whereas London has 1.96 ha of open space per 1,000 people, and New York 2.16 ha, Mumbai has only 0.04 ha of open space available for every 1,000 persons.

The following year he exhibited his open spaces map and his plans and designs for the regeneration of existing and the creation of new open spaces at the *National Gallery of Modern Art* in Mumbai. Accompanying the exhibition, a publication was prepared entitled *Open Mumbai: Re-envisioning the City and its Open Spaces.*

The exhibition and book outline ideas to improve the city's riverfronts, stands of mangroves, beaches, ponds, lakes, tanks and wetlands. They also outline plans for the creation of new public parks, the improvement of railway stations, and the renovation of avenues and roads to improve pedestrian movement.

The plans show a great variety in subjects, but share that they are modest in design, fairly simple to execute, and aim to democratize public spaces. All in all, PK Das strongly believes that with some collective effort Mumbai can double its open spaces – making the city a more liveable place. He tells us that the exhibition was covered in practically every newspaper published in the city, and that 'politicians' response was great'. He is a little apprehensive, though, quickly adding: 'We have to see what can be sustained'.

LEARNING FROM...

His experience as an activist architect has taught PK Das many lessons. One of the most important ones regards 'the role of the architects and other professionals in planning and development for the public interest'.[4] He and Munshi put it as follows: 'The support lent by professionals to (...) citizen movements is often very inadequate. They are trained to work with clients or patrons and seldom collectives such as citizens' associations. Much of the time there is a barrier between the professional, who prepares the design and the plans, the agency involved in implementing it, and the people whom it benefits. The people and their needs are seldom taken into account by the professional in the design prepared for projects of public interest. In Bandra a very different process emerged. An initial design prepared by PK Das was used to stimulate citizens' interest. People then began to understand the different social dimensions of the project – the way it would change their lives – and wanted to get involved. Regular discussions gave the process momentum.'[5]

All in all, he strongly feels that 'the architect needs to undertake a larger responsibility' than usually is the case 'to play the role of an activist and to relate design with larger and more important factors of social and political importance'.[6] His numerous works in Mumbai are an example not just of how that is done, but also of what grand things can be achieved in this way.

1 PK DAS AND INDRA MUNSHI. 2011. *On The Waterfront. Reclaiming Mumbai's Open Spaces.* Mumbai: PK Das & Associates and Mumbai Waterfronts Center. pp. 6 and 10.
2 Idem. p.58.
3 Idem. p.68.
4 Idem. p.77.
5 Idem. p.77.
6 Idem. p.77.

BANDRA BANDSTAND, BANDRA

CITIZENS
USV

OPEN MUMBAI PLAN

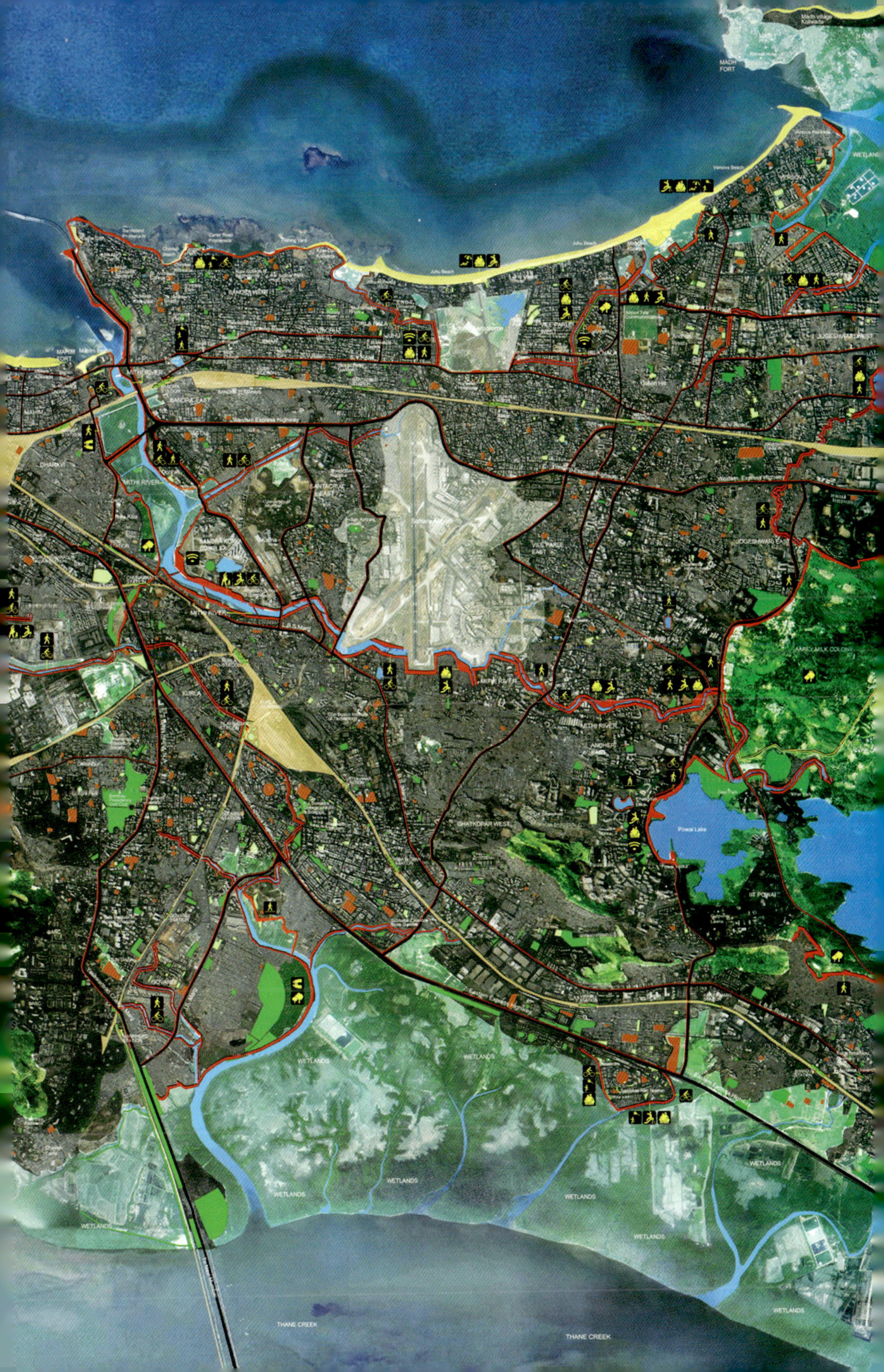

MADH FORT
Juhu Beach
MITHI RIVER
Sahara Airport
AAREY MILK COLONY
GHATKOPAR WEST
Powai Lake
IIT POWAI
WETLANDS
THANE CREEK

NULLAHS, BEFORE AND AFTER

FOOD COURT AT JUHU BEACH

MY MUMBAI
PK DAS

MUMBAI IS SPECIAL BECAUSE

Mumbai is special because of its history of incredible social and political movements. These movements shaped and defined the city. Ambedkar's Dalit movement started in the city in the nineteenth century, and challenged the basic structures of the Indian caste system. It is also the birthplace of the *Indian National Congress*, which led the Independence movement from the late nineteenth century onwards. Mahatma Gandhi launched his Quit India campaign against British rule in the city in 1942. But also after Independence many political, social, and citizen movements have been started here. The Workers Union and Rights movement, for example, who started the first trade unions in Mumbai. I have engaged actively and enthusiastically with a variety of movements in social debates. And over the years have become part of several democratic movements for justice and community welfare as well.

THIS CAN BE IMPROVED

The city can improve in the field of participatory planning and governance. There is an urgent need to integrate planning and architecture with larger democratic movements. As of now exclusive developments promote the concept of gated communities and leave the city underdeveloped. Mega-malls are built for the elite, and health departments encourage huge hospitals with luxurious facilities at high prices. Even new educational complexes that are constructed are meant primarily for the rich.

MY FAVOURITE PLACE

It is not one place in particular, but a stretch of places: Mumbai's incredible waterfronts. The larger democratic movement that I am part of wants to reclaim the waterfronts as a public space. Although Mumbai is a city on the water, the waterfronts have never been considered an integral part of the city's land mass. I am looking forward to seeing a Mumbai where the waterfronts are protected, integrated with the development of the city, and added as quality open spaces for all citizens.

MY FAVOURITE RESTAURANT

The Irani cafés of the city. These are disappearing now, and making place for fancier restaurants and pubs. They used to provide a humble space for informal meetings and discussions. They were originally opened in the nineteenth century by Persian immigrants and serve Mumbai classics as *bun maska* [bread with butter], special *chai* [tea], *berry pulao* [a sweet rice dish] and *kheema pav* [bread with spicy minced mutton].

MY FAVOURITE LANDMARK

Land's End, Bandra. This is the southernmost tip of Bandra, and is adorned with a fort from the seventeenth century, which we have restored.

THE BEST PLACE TO RELAX

My house.

IF ONE THING COULD BE DEMOLISHED IT WOULD BE

Exclusivity and colonization of public assets. At present the method of the government is mostly to privatize developments. In this way public assets are taken away from the public to the private sphere. The government is backing out of its responsibility to directly develop social welfare projects. Instead it wants to facilitate private agencies to boost developments.

WHAT WE CAN LEARN FROM MUMBAI

That a city has opportunity to forge collective endeavours.

THE ARCHITECT AS A GUARDIAN OF THE PUBLIC REALM

BRINDA SOMAYA

Brinda Somaya (1949) completed her Bachelor's of Architecture at the Sir J.J. College of Architecture and obtained her Master of Arts from Smith College in Northampton, Massachusetts in the USA. In 2012 she received an Honorary Doctorate from her alma mater.

Upon returning to India in 1978, together with her sister Ranjini Kalappa, she started her own firm: *Somaya and Kalappa Consultants*. Their work spans corporate, industrial and institutional projects, as well as building conservation and design of public spaces. At present *Somaya and Kalappa Consultants* has two offices in India and around fifty employees and has received a wide range of national and international awards for their designs.

Somaya's passion for conservation is reflected in her professional portfolio, but also in her activities for the Mumbai Urban Heritage Conservation Committee, on which she served two terms, and the *HECAR Foundation*, an organization she co-founded in 1999 to educate the public about architecture, heritage conservation and urban issues through talks, publications and seminars.

Brinda has lectured extensively on a wide range of topics in India and abroad. In 2000 she organized *Women in Architecture*, a conference, exhibition and publication about female architects in South Asia.

When we ask her to describe her philosophy as an architect, Brinda Somaya refers to Jane Jacobs' 1992 publication *Systems of Survival*, where the *grande dame* of Urban Studies describes the world as being ruled by two separate moral paradigms underlying the work and actions of people: the commercial and the guardian. 'Architects need to be part of the guardian paradigm', Brinda explains. 'They need to guard the public realm and interest.' Throughout her career she has lived this philosophy by merging architecture, conservation and social equity in the projects she undertook. 'From the very beginning part of my work has revolved around conservation and restoration, and part around social projects.'

HERITAGE CONSERVATION & RENOVATION

'The renovation projects I undertook were very diverse', Brinda explains while showing us close-up photographs from the *St Thomas Cathedral* she restored in 2003. 'Sometimes the original use of a building was maintained, such as in the case of the *Cathedral* and the three *Cathedral & John Connon Schools* in Fort, Mumbai. Here we had to seamlessly introduce the schools' current requirements without disturbing the original design. We wanted to prove that old buildings, in this case dating from the early eighteenth century and the late nineteenth century, could fulfil today's needs. We added new features to the schools, such as an extension of the staircase and an additional floor, and we repaired and uncovered existing features that had been bricked up and plastered over. For example, we repaired the bird and flower carvings on the columns, and uncovered the original niches in the corridors.'

In other projects, buildings, and spaces the functions were radically altered. 'An old sewage pumping station we are working on currently will become an arts and crafts centre. And a former factory shed was transformed into an educational institute.'

NOT A HOBBY FOR THE ELITE

Brinda is not just concerned with heritage projects as a practising architect, but also as a policy advisor and advocate. 'I've been on the Mumbai Urban Heritage Conservation Committee for last ten years, I was part of *Mumbai's Initiative for the Protection and Improvement of Streets and Public Spaces*, and of *INTACH*, the *Indian National Trust for Art and Cultural Heritage*. In 1999 I co-founded the *HECAR Foundation*, which is an acronym for Heritage Education Conservation Architecture and Restoration. Many buildings are falling apart in South Mumbai and we have attempted to save and revitalize some of them. We try to educate the public about architecture, heritage conservation and urban issues through talks, publications and seminars.' She stresses that gentrification and heritage conservation are not merely hobbies for the elite. 'Upgrading old neighbourhoods benefits the poor as well', she argues. 'They too enjoy the sight of well-designed and well-restored buildings. It gives people, all people, a sense of history. They do not go to Navi Mumbai to admire a new gated community being constructed there, but they do come down to the *Gateway of India* on Sunday to admire the old buildings in that area and to enjoy the plaza spaces.'

PUBLIC-PRIVATE PARTNERSHIPS

Social projects form another important part of her work. 'I have clients who are big industrialists and we do big commercial buildings for them, but these clients like to do other types of work as well. For example, they want to spend part of their profits on philanthropy and build a hospital. Or they want to help create a new public space in the city.'

The *Colaba Woods* project provides a good example of the latter. 'The *Tata Electric Company*, the local *Lions Club* and the citizens of Colaba and Cuffe Parade came together and leased four acres of land on the southern tip of Mumbai from the Municipal Corporation. The land was used as a garbage dump and they wanted to transform it into a park. We couldn't afford a landscape architect, but we succeeded nevertheless and together transformed it into a green forest amidst the concrete jungle that surrounds it. Today it is the green lung of the locality, and accessible to anyone. This was the first public-private partnership for a public space in the city and it set a precedent', Brinda says proudly. 'Similar small parks, co-funded with private money, have come up all over the city.'

REBUILDING A VILLAGE

Another example of a social building project by *Somaya & Kalappa Consultants* that was co-funded with corporate money was the rebuilding of a village in Kutch district, in Gujarat. In 2001, a massive earthquake destroyed many houses and buildings in the region. 'One of our oldest clients wanted to take action, help the earthquake victims', says Brinda. 'Together with an NGO that was familiar with the area, *SHRUJAN*, we identified a village where we would work. Our requirement was that the villagers themselves wanted to work *with* us, rather than us to work *for* them. We wanted them to be involved in the project. We selected Bhadli village, located only 40 kilometres west of Bhuj, the epicentre of the earthquake. Almost 90 percent of the houses in the village were destroyed. The houses that had not collapsed showed major cracks.'

'We went there several times to show our drawings and gather their feedback. The government had supplied modules, which were adequate and functional, but not designed in accordance with the specific needs of the people. Certain specific features, such as the need for verandas and for extra space around doorframes to allow for the local tradition of decorating these with designs made out of lime, clay and mirror were not given importance. The underlying character of the village was also not incorporated into their designs. With the feedback of the villagers we drew new models.'

'We provided the materials and paid the villagers for their labour', Brinda continues. 'Their involvement built their confidence and they were really part of the rebuilding process. We were just the catalysts and facilitators.'

THE ESPLANADE PROJECT

When we ask about particular Mumbai projects she is currently involved in, Brinda shows press material about *The Esplanade Project*, an initiative to give more space to pedestrians in South Mumbai. Space is scarce in Mumbai and one solution to serve the ever-growing number of cars is to build roads on top of other roads; flyovers as they call them locally. The next step is to make the road not two but three levels high. According to Brinda this is the wrong approach: 'I believe that the moment you build a flyover over another flyover the city is doomed. And we have just reached that point. Public transport is neglected, and the people who use public transport are forgotten. Every day *lakhs* of people [a *lakh* is 100,000] come out of the railway stations, and they are herded like animals. To improve this situation we developed a plan together with urban planners for new underpasses and plazas. We worked hard on our design, had exhibitions of our plans, and got huge public support. We have shown our plans to the government officials, to the railways. People who supported us ask us regularly what happened to our plans. Unfortunately we encountered a major lack of political will to act. It is typical for citizen-concerned projects like this: lots of people know about it and think it is all good, but there are fewer money-making possibilities, and thus no interest. Our plan respects the millions of people who come by train. All we can say is that we haven't given up on it. In India you can't give up.'

BUREAUCRACY

A bottom-up approach of listening to the needs of the end-users, of the common people, and involving them in design decisions is characteristic for Brinda Somaya's approach. 'Unless there is participation, and a will coming from the people to use, develop or save a building or a space, nothing is going to change', she emphasizes. Yet, as became clear from *The Esplanade Project*, to create change in the city, ensuring citizens' participation and funds from well-wishers is not sufficient. Cooperation from the local authorities is crucial as well. In every project we discuss with her this difficulty of dealing with the government surfaces.

'To get things done here you either need a powerful political connection, or happen to find a bureaucrat who is committed', Brinda explains. 'If you find a bureaucrat in a key position with vision, ability, integrity and commitment, you can work fast. We had a few good ones here, and some of the heritage conservation projects we were able to undertake are thanks to them. When we were working on *Colaba Woods* we were also lucky to encounter a far-thinking official in the municipality.' She sometimes wonders what the city would look like if only all the officials were as 'good and courageous' though. 'Unfortunately they operate within a system that seems designed to confuse you, and they are often rather inaccessible for common citizens. When trying to get things done, you always need to go through a network, rather than just rely on your rights as a citizen.'

WOMEN IN ARCHITECTURE

In 2000 Brinda organized a conference entitled *Women in Architecture*. 'When my sister and I started our practice over three decades ago there were not many women with studios. Our mother always taught us to try and be independent, to pay our "rent on earth" doing public projects. And that is what we did.' After two decades of hard work Brinda became curious about other women in architecture in South Asia. Were there any? What work were they doing? What could be learned from them? 'It was 1990 and I sent letters around', she recalls, 'but I did not get a single response. It seemed there simply were no women-run practices at that time.' Ten years later things had changed. 'The response to my second round of letters was overwhelming and I decided to organize a conference and exhibit the work of female South Asian architects.'

'The intention was not to organize a conference on gender issues. It had to be a celebration of the work of women. So I insisted that all papers and exhibition material were about the built form. It consisted of women who had upgraded slums, conserved heritage buildings, improved urban spaces and built private and public buildings of every possible type.' The conference was a success. The exhibition travelled the world, and a book, *Women In Architecture. An Emancipated Place*, in which some twenty female architects were profiled, was published the same year.

Although no follow-up conference has been organized, Brinda remains involved in the issue of women and architecture. Wondering why so many girls take up architecture in college and so few start a practice, she realized it had to do with a lack of confidence. 'Many girls, after college, take a break to start a family', she explains. 'Over time they lose confidence about their skills as an architect. We started classes to rebuild this confidence, classes to brush up their knowledge and their design skills. And to our great satisfaction we found that after only three months these women were back on track and ready to start working.'

LEARNING FROM...

Although she feels that all architects around the world should be part of the guardian paradigm, Brinda stresses that within that realm an architect in India has different obligations than an architect in the West. She explains: 'The problem is that we tell ourselves that our profession is the same, and that our location does not matter. But it does matter, and our profession isn't the same. We all have responsibilities towards our cities, societies, but these responsibilities change from country to country and from context to context. As a doctor in India you encounter dengue, malaria, chickenpox and – until recently – polio with a certain regularity. A doctor in the Unites States may not see any of these during his entire career. For me being an Indian architect in India means, for example, that I want to include the expertise of local craftsmen in my work, like the local artisans, weavers, metalworkers, and provide them with work. So if you ask me what may foreign architects, in collaborating with me on projects, have learned from me, I'd say I helped them to understand the Indian ethos and what it means to work as an architect in India.'

OLD YACHT CLUB, COLABA

NALANDA INTERNATIONAL SCHOOL, VADODARA, GUJARAT

OVAL MAIDAN, CHURCHGATE

MY MUMBAI
BRINDA SOMAYA

MUMBAI IS SPECIAL BECAUSE
It is home for me. I moved here at the age of eight and I have seen the city change, the good and the bad. But I was there when it happened and I can relate with the city.

THIS CAN BE IMPROVED
Everything. But I think most importantly what needs to change is the attitude towards the average person who struggles to live in the city.

MY FAVOURITE PLACE
The sea. I love the fact that we are an island. When I go away I miss the sea the most. The infinity. And because the city has the sea we can live and breathe here. We have the breeze, the expanse. This gives us a sense of space, visually and mentally, in a city that otherwise lacks space more than anything else.

MY FAVOURITE RESTAURANT
Indigo Deli in Colaba is definitely a favourite. We have a farmhouse in Alibaug and when we go there we often pick up sandwiches from *Indigo* before taking the boat. Another favourite is *Kailash Parbat*: they have the best *pani puri* [small crispy round breads filled with a mixture of flavoured water, potatoes, peas, onions, chutney and spices].

MY FAVOURITE LANDMARK
The datum line marker in Horniman Circle that tells you that you are standing at mean sea level of the city. I always look at it when I walk past it. It marks a historical centre, and is reasonably well preserved.

THE BEST PLACE TO RELAX
The boardwalk along the sea in Navy Nagar. It is not publicly accessible, you need to be a member of *The United Services Club*. You can walk almost to the lighthouse and back in total peace, just surrounded by the sea.

IF ONE THING COULD BE DEMOLISHED IT WOULD BE
In the area where my office is, Ballard Estate, there is one tall building that is totally out of sync with its surroundings in terms of mass and height. It is the building of the *Port Trust*. That should be torn down, just as any other building that does not respect its context.

MY FAVOURITE MUMBAI BOOK
The Trees of Mumbai (2006) written by Marselin Almeida and Naresh Chaturvedi, and published by the *Bombay Natural History Society*. It is a beautiful little book that gives the names, pictures and a short description of all the trees that grow in Mumbai. It is amazing what a variety we have!

MY CHOICE OF TRANSPORTATION
When I was young I used to love the trains and the buses. But now that I am a grandmother, I prefer to take the car.

WHAT WE CAN LEARN FROM MUMBAI
We can learn from the spirit of the people of this city. They are facing so many difficulties, yet through this there is an energy and vitality that comes through, a sense of aspiration for the future, a will to dream. Of course, it is easy for me to say this from my privileged position, but I can still see it and learn from it.

THE CITY IS YOUR CANVAS

THE WALL PROJECT

Nitya Amarnath (1982) is a textile designer.
Chaitanya Modak (1978) is a communication designer.
Dhanya Pilo (1981) is a filmmaker and visual artist.
Shazeb Shaikh (1983) is in advertising.

A spontaneous plan to liven up a wall in their compound, thought up by some friends one Sunday afternoon in 2006, was the start of one of the most intriguing beautification projects Mumbai has seen in recent years: *The Wall Project.*

Dhanya Pilo, Nitya Amarnath, Chaitanya Modak, Shazeb Shaikh and several others lamented the fact that they hardly worked with their hands anymore. They decided to take up a brush to paint the wall. When neighbours came along to see what was happening, and joined in, adding paintings of their own, they planned to gather again two weeks later to make a second mural on the outside of the building. 'We had so much fun that we wanted to keep doing it', Nitya recalls.

'Soon we got requests for paintings coming from all corners. We spread the word around the neighbourhood that if people wanted their wall livened up they should paint it white. That way we would know which walls were okay to paint on', says Dhanya. 'That happened on a great scale', Shazeb adds. 'It took on a life of its own.'

PRINCIPLES

They think that apart from the paintings themselves, the two main principles by which they work contributed to their success: asking for permission and refraining from religious and political messages.

'We figured we best go ahead only if we have permission. What we make is not graffiti. It is not vandalism. It is public art, street art. We promise the wall owners that if they don't like the end result, we remove it. But that has never happened so far.' It helps that in Mumbai not many regulations exist with regard to public spaces. Unlike in the Netherlands, where you have a so-called *welstandscommissie* regulating everything regarding buildings and the public domain, in Mumbai there is no monitoring body concerned with the beauty of urban space and buildings.

Of all the paintings that were done, they know of only one that has been removed. 'A neighbour was afraid the beautified wall would appreciate the street. He was hoping for redevelopment of the buildings into high-rises, and with the area becoming more beautiful he was afraid this would not happen. So he destroyed the painting', Dhanya explains.

Their second pillar is 'no controversial messages'. No politics, no religion – even direct social messages are avoided. 'We were once asked to make an anti-tobacco mural, but we declined. We make *art*, not adverts or campaigns. If our art inspires people to live more healthily and quit smoking, well that is great, but we are not going to write it on a wall.'

TULSI PIPE ROAD

About two years after their first mural they received an email from the municipal corporation. 'They asked us to come to their office', Nitya recalls. 'We had no idea what to expect and were a little afraid that they would tell us to stop painting.' It turned out the local government wanted exactly the opposite: they wanted to help them paint *more* walls. 'They offered to pay for our paint, and asked us where we wanted to start. We had a long list of municipal walls we wanted to do, but it was clear which one would be the first', says Dhanya.

This led to what is no doubt their most famous project among the citizenry of Mumbai: the two-kilometre long wall along Tulsi Pipe Road in Mahim and Dadar. On *Facebook* they announced a date and time for people to come and paint. About five hundred people showed up. 'Apart from these people some others also joined simply when driving by', Nitya says. "They saw us, got curious, stopped, got inspired and took up a brush! It was great. People from all walks of life worked on this wall: professional artists, children, students, families, young, old, rich, poor.'

Those who felt unconfident about their skills or lacked ideas could get help from an artist, but overall it was emphasized that the event was not necessarily about the quality of the painting and that people should paint what they felt like. 'Ultimately this wall was about the community experience', says Shazeb.

MORE THAN ART

Although *The Wall Project* started apolitical and still avoids obvious social messages, their work unintentionally did become more than mere *l'art pour l'art*. They have noticed interesting side effects of their activities, or 'butterfly effects' as they prefer to call them. People taking an interest in and caring about public property, for example. 'The paint on Tulsi Pipe Road was not dry yet or some guy came that night and plastered advertisements for a new Bollywood film over it. The next day the media were all over it. We decided to keep quiet. To let the participants react, to let them take ownership. They did. And how! The rage was such that in the end the filmmakers, including the hero of the film, made a public apology for it', Nitya says.

There are more stories like this. Shazeb shares: 'One man who helped painting the wall drove by it one day to see a guy peeing on it. He stepped out of his car and chased him! Have you ever seen that in India? Someone reprimanding some stranger for urinating on a wall?'

Another change they have seen over the years is that painting is seen less and less as something you let other people – workers, artists – do for you. 'Of course, good research is needed to see if there is a direct link, but it is interesting to notice how advertisements for paint have changed', Dhanya says. 'There are several campaigns now where you see Bollywood actors smilingly taking up a brush to paint their living room. That is really something new.'

REQUESTS

Over the years all kinds of people have approached *The Wall Project*: advertisement agencies, event organizers, housing societies, schools. The mural artists have remained selective in who they want to work with as they value their independence and do not want to be 'used'. Often they decline and they only cooperate when a project really fits their ideas on what *The Wall Project* should be about. Such as when an NGO that had adopted part of a slum in Andheri approached them with the story that they were transforming the local garbage dump into a playground. The wall along the plot could use some paint. As the murals were to be done together with the children, the artists decided to participate. 'This ownership, we feel, is one of the most important things. It makes them proud. It makes them care for the wall. And it is a way to express themselves', Dhanya explains.

OTHER PROJECTS

Busy with their respective careers in textile design, filmmaking, interior design, and advertising and activities related to *The Wall Project*, Dhanya, Nitya, Shazeb and Chaitanya feel that lately they have too little time to actually paint. But that doesn't mean that new paintings are no longer appearing in the city. Ranjit Dahiya and Tony Peter started the *Bollywood Art Project* and make murals 'inspired by the seventy-year-old design tradition of hand-painted Bollywood posters'. Their stunning works include two twenty by fifteen foot (4.6 x 6 m) murals on Chapel Road in Bandra and a thirty by twenty foot (6.1 x 6 m) painting in Khar.

And others too have taken up a brush. 'In fact, the questions on how to go about finding and painting walls from outsiders became so frequent that we decided to answer the most commonly asked questions on our website', Shazeb says. Their FAQ section reads like a handbook for how to make murals in Mumbai.

They are not sure how many people are painting. They do not monitor what is being made everywhere in the city. They simply hope that those who were inspired by their murals will develop it further and not limit themselves to copying street artists in the West. 'There are some guys now doing plain graffiti. We hope that those who take this up will develop their own style.'

THE FUTURE

In the meantime, *The Wall Project* people are working on an audio tour and conduct workshops with art students and students from other schools. Their work will be featured on free post cards that are distributed in coffee shops around the country, and their paintings feature frequently as a backdrop in video clips and photo shoots.

A lot has changed over the years since that Sunday afternoon, and not just the way the city looks. But what remains is the pleasure and surprise of the interaction with people on the streets during their work. Says Dhanya: 'This city is expensive to live in. For a lot of people here days consist of a struggle to make ends meet, to simply earn a livelihood. People are busy with work, with education. And then they see this bunch of people doing something for the city, for the community, for the area. Taking the city's walls as their canvas. We want to be independent and pay for the paint from our own pockets. There is no logic to that, they feel. It doesn't make sense. And *that* is really exciting.'

The The Wall Project *paintings can be found all over Mumbai. Particularly good places to see them are Tulsi Pipe Road, starting from Mahim Railway station, Chapel Rd in Bandra, and the by-lanes of Colaba Causeway, such as Pasta Lane.*

MURAL ON CHAPEL RD, BANDRA

MURAL ON TULSI PIPE RD, MAHIM

hort,
but
it
is
جشن امام احمد رضا
PAN CA
Rs. 170/-
KUSHWAHA ENTERP
AADHAR APPLI
&
PAN CA
Rs 100/-

MACHIMAR VILLAGE, COLABA

MY MUMBAI
THE WALL PROJECT

MUMBAI IS SPECIAL BECAUSE

Chaitanya: Mumbai is special because it lives 'inside out'. Everything is out on the street. There is so much chaos. You can see through it. There is so much activity, and all the people you see are all extremely different, yet they live so close together.
Dhanya: Mumbai allows you to get exactly whatever you want. For example, it is possible to get a single piece of something that is normally sold in bulk. Customization is something we are very good at here.
Nitya: The sea. We may not use it much, but it gives us a possibility to see the horizon. It is a point of relief; even if many people are also very scared of it as most of Mumbai is build on reclamations.

THIS CAN BE IMPROVED

Dhanya: Accountability and governance.
Chaitanya: We could use a forced holiday. A day when everything is closed: shops, malls, cinemas, except public parks.

MY FAVOURITE RESTAURANT

Nitya: *The Tea Centre* next to the Churchgate railway station and *Soul Fry* at the Pali Market in Bandra. It is particularly worth checking it out if you like fish.
Chaitanya: Zitar in Powai. I was involved in the design of it.
Shazeb: Leopold Cafe in Colaba. It has been around forever and never really changes.

MY FAVOURITE LANDMARK

Shazeb: *Flora Fountain*, because I grew up in that area, and because it is still sort of quiet there. There are hardly ever any traffic jams.
Dhanya: Chapel Road in Bandra. I used to live there, and it is where many of our paintings are.

THE BEST PLACE TO RELAX

Chaitanya: Carter Road, Bandra. In 2002 the promenade along the Arabian Sea was opened to public. It's a great place for a stroll, to stare at the sea.
Dhanya: On a sailboat in the harbour.
Nitya: In the front seat on the upper deck of the old *BEST* buses.

IF ONE THING COULD BE DEMOLISHED IT WOULD BE

Dhanya: Billboards with political faces and houses with glass facades.

IF NOT MUMBAI THEN

Nitya: Copenhagen maybe.
Chaitanya: Delhi, more and more is happening there in the art scene.

WHAT WE CAN LEARN FROM MUMBAI

Dhanya: Patience. And that no is never an option. There is always a way around the rules to make something happen. The positive attitude of 'make do and make happen'.
Nitya: Spontaneity. I never need to call my friends a *month* ahead to plan a dinner. I just drop in and everyone finds that normal.

SOCIALLY AND ENVIRONMENTALLY CONSCIOUS ARCHITECTURE

ROBERT VERRIJT & SHEFALI BALWANI

Robert Verrijt (1979) completed a Master's degree in Architecture at the TU Delft in the Netherlands. During his studies, as part of an exchange programme, he spent several months in India with the Centre for Environmental Planning and Technology (CEPT) in Ahmedabad. After graduating he joined *MICD Associates* in Colombo, Sri Lanka; this is the office of Channa Daswatte, one of Geoffrey Bawa's protégés. His work included renovations, houses, high-end condominiums, boutique resorts and hotels.

Since moving to Mumbai in 2006 he has taught part-time at KRVIA and he became affiliated as Visiting Faculty to the Balwant Sheth School of Architecture, in Mumbai. He co-founded *Architecture Brio* with his wife Shefali Balwani in 2006.

Shefali Balwani (1978) completed a Bachelor's of Architecture at the CEPT in Ahmedabad. During her studies, as part of an exchange programme, she spent several months in the Netherlands at TU Delft. Upon graduation she joined the office of Rahul Mehrotra, *Rahul Mehrotra Associates*, in Mumbai. Later she moved to Sri Lanka to work for Channa Daswatte at *MICD Associates*. She was responsible for a variety of projects such as the part refurbishment of Geoffrey Bawa's *Lighthouse Hotel.*

In 2006 she returned to her native Mumbai and co-founded *Architecture Brio* with her husband Robert Verrijt.

She is Indian. He is Dutch. Shefali Balwani and Robert Verrijt met twelve years ago while they were studying architecture at TU Delft. Subsequently they worked together in Sri Lanka, and in 2006 they started their own firm, *BRIO Architecture*, in Mumbai. Their office is located in a quaint heritage building in the leafy western suburb of Khar.

NOT JUST ELITES

To situate their own work, and to explain what kind of firm theirs is, Robert and Shefali share their thoughts on the architecture scene in the city. 'The two extremes of the spectrum are taken up by the commercial companies on one side and the quality-driven firms on the other', Robert explains. 'The commercial companies work almost factory-like and under a constant pressure of: "Have it ready tomorrow!" The quality-driven firms work in a small niche. We feel very close to these quality firms, but we would not feel comfortable if we would only work on exclusive private projects, as they usually do. See, for these niche firms the only way to make absolutely sure that everything goes according to their quality standards is to be on top of everything. They literally have to keep track of each nail that is used at their construction sites. If they do not monitor so rigorously they can be sure it is not a stainless steel nail that goes in. The companies that can have such complete control generally have to work without budget or a timeline. As for us, we are ambitious and take architecture very seriously. But we want to do projects that touch large sections of society, not just the elites.'

BUTTERFLIES

Their portfolio shows that their commitment to societal projects is very real indeed. For example, in recent years, they designed a master plan, a learning pavilion and a staff dormitory for the Indian education NGO *Magic Bus* in Karjat, near Mumbai. They also worked on a Biodiversity Training Institute (together with *fUSE Studio* from the Netherlands) in Sikkim, the mountainous state in North India bordered by Nepal, China and Bhutan. And in the same state they have just completed their design for *The Butterfly Reserve*.

While showing us images of the breathtaking site in Sikkim, Robert says, 'Currently around 690 types of butterflies can be found in this spectacular region. However, their habitat is under threat: from climate change, the invasion of non-native plants, infrastructural developments and urbanization. *The Butterfly Reserve* was started to provide a "safe haven" for butterflies, and to create awareness about the importance of butterflies for the eco-system. The project reserves seventy-five acres [30 ha] of land for the winged creatures, and opens a small portion of nine acres [3 ha] to the public.'

Robert and Shefali were asked to design the pavilions from which visitors can view the butterflies and the entrance structure of the reserve. They studied local building techniques and blended these in their designs with modern techniques. 'The pavilions consist of lightweight timber frame structures on light steel columns', Robert explains. 'The "wattle & daub" timber frame structure is a common vernacular building method in Sikkim. It builds on centuries of knowledge and is suited to the climatic conditions of the region. What we did was change its traditional appearance by cladding the frames with local timber roofing shingles, mounted like the scales on a butterfly's wing.'

NON-INVASIVE ARCHITECTURE

While their work for *The Butterfly Reserve* showcases their societal commitment, it also provides a good example of Robert and Shefali's architectural vision. Each and every project they start from the premise that they want to 'intervene in the existing landscape in a conscious way'. Their aim is to create non-invasive architecture for their sites. In Shefali's words: 'We try to be conscious about our environment, as each site has a unique design. We do not feel we have to place our stamp on each site. We look at what the environment needs.'

The butterfly interpretation pavilions are thus blended in with their environs. 'They flank the "butterfly enclosures", areas enclosed by nets, where the butterflies are protected from predators and can breed undisturbed', says Shefali. 'These enclosures are dispersed throughout the landscape, and because of the design and the location of the enclosures and the pavilions, the visitors are drawn into the natural habitat of the butterfly.'

Robert and Shefali feel close to the work of Sri Lankan architect Geoffrey Bawa, for whom they worked prior to starting their own firm in Mumbai. 'Bawa was known for working in beautiful places.

He used to say, "I want to see my surroundings through the building. What I see when I look out of the window, that is important." His work and his lessons definitely influence the direction of our practice', Shefali tells.

In fact, they take his approach one step further, as they do not just give the environment priority while designing, but also during the construction phase of their work. Thus, for *The Butterfly Reserve*, they made sure that all the pavilions were prefabricated, to minimize construction disturbance on site.

MONEY MATTERS

One thing we wonder about is how lucrative it is to work in Mumbai as an architect. Robert and Shefali provide us with some insight and share that the fee they can charge depends on the type of project. 'With very luxury private villa projects your fee could be as much as 1/5th of the total cost of construction. But with a middle-class residential structure, a public building, or a building designed for a large-scale developer the fees drastically decrease. It could be 1/20th or 1/30th of the cost. The general rule is that the larger the project becomes, the more repetition there is in a design, the lower the fee for the architect will be.'

To enable comparison with the Netherlands, we ask what building an average middle-class home in India would cost and what you would make on this as an architect. We suggest a semi-detached house of some 200 square metres. In the Netherlands building a house like that would cost about EUR 400,000. The architect would maybe earn EUR 50,000 on such a project, which amounts to about 12.5% of the total cost. 'In India', Robert says, 'you can construct the same for around 150,000 euros. The architect would expect to take home around 1/10th of the cost as his fee, so say about 15,000 euros.'

Shefali and Robert stress that differing fee structures notwithstanding, some aspects of running an architecture firm in Mumbai and in the Netherlands are very much the same. For example, renting an office space in a city where rents are sky-high puts a heavy burden on any company, as does purchasing the necessary software licenses. 'All in all, it is the salary of the staff where the difference is', Robert explains. 'Salaries are much lower here, and employers usually do not need to pay all kinds of fees for pension funds, social insurances, and health care as they do in the Netherlands.'

BEST OF BOTH WORLDS: STEPS & DETAILS

Over the years Robert and Shefali adapted their way of working to use the best of both worlds: they want to maintain a high control over quality, while remaining within reasonable budgets and timelines. To achieve this they have learned to work 'in steps'. 'We request the builder to make one element at the time and to do it as best as he can. If we don't like it, he needs to redo it before we give our go-ahead. This way we have a standard for the rest of the work that we can refer to and make him accountable.' They found it the easiest way to control the quality of the output on site while working in an environment with lesser standardization than in the Netherlands.

They also learned how detailed their drawings need to be, and – more importantly – which details can be dispensed with, and which not. 'Although local clients, builders and consultants are not very image-oriented, we purposely still draw many of the details', Robert explains. 'Other architects may go to the construction site, sketch on the wall, and explain it on the spot to the carpenter. That sounds very romantic, but we found that for us it is hard to control the quality of the outcome this way. So we are learning on the go: which details we should elaborate on, and which we need not spend so much time on.'

Their insistence on drawing details has reaped success not just in how their final products have turned out, but also in the acquisition of new projects. 'We were working on an apartment for which we made quite an extensive drawing and had researched all details. One day we got a phone call from a potential client. He had heard from one of our technical consultants that our drawings were so elaborate. If we could meet, he asked. The end result is that we are now working for him on a new project. So in this case it was our drawings that got noticed and generated new business', Robert says.

PLATFORM

If they miss something in Mumbai it is a critical platform of architects. 'Young architects with good ideas and vision hardly get the opportunity to build on a large scale, to share their ideas, and to prove themselves', Robert says. 'Those who have built acres and acres of campuses, apartment buildings and headquarters merely do what is asked of them by developers. These architects have the ability to influence, to create change in the world of architecture, but they often lack the guts to stand up for themselves.'

The lack of reflection, of activism, and of criticism is partially because it is not part of architects' education, Robert thinks. 'The task of students here is to listen and memorize. They are not encouraged or supported to develop their own vision.' Another cause, he thinks, is the lack of time local architects have had for contemplation. 'In the 1970s and 1980s there wasn't much to do here. Then, in the 1990s, all of a sudden the developments went so fast that there was no time for reflection. Nobody had a good story really. No one had time to think of one.'

MISSED CHANCES

Talking about the various projects they dream of doing in Mumbai, Robert mentions a few instances of what he calls 'missed chances'. 'I learned about this plan for a new building to replace the Pali Market in Bandra, for instance', he says. 'The plans are stalled for the moment, but when I saw the designs I wondered: Why create a market with only high-end residences on top? Why not make a building with different programmes in one? Why not integrate good parking solutions in the plan, but also functions for the people who live or work in the area, or who come and visit? Why not make the building serve the neighbourhood rather then feed on it?'

'Another example is the otherwise quite interesting building of the *Bombay Arts Society* in Bandra. You can tell that they invested a great effort to make something special. But when you take a closer look you find that the building lacks smart solutions for that particular location, and for that programme. It is a missed chance as it *could* have meant so much more for the city. It *could* have been a meeting point for different communities and classes. If only its public function was more emphasized by its design, and location.' When encouraged to come up with a better location, Robert starts to brainstorm: 'Why not as a pavilion in the middle of *Bandra Talao*, the large water basin near the station? I can imagine you make footbridges connecting the two sides of the pond and the building, and make it a passageway.'

Summarizing, Robert argues that discussions about architecture – when held at all – remain too superficial. Particularly the question 'For *whom* is this particular design or plan better?' is neglected, he feels. 'You can create a wonderful residential complex, marvellous in design and construction, but what I want to ask is: "Is it also a good building for Mumbai?" I feel that question should be much higher on the agenda than it is now – and probably higher on the agenda than it needs to be in the Netherlands – because of the population density, and because of the inequalities in the city.'

LEARNING FROM...

All in all, for Robert the vibrancy of the city compensates for the lack of vibrancy in the architecture world. 'Of course, not all the things you learn are directly useful when you go back to the Netherlands. But there is nevertheless a lot to discover and learn here for Dutch architects', he says. 'Mumbai requires or challenges you to think innovatively. The complexity, the multi-layeredness, the diversity. Society is moving all the time. And that keeps you sharp. Mumbai asks for your engagement, you can't just be a by-stander. It's never boring here. It's never easy. This city is a challenge, but a fun one.'

MAGIC BUS LEARNING PAVILION, KARJAT

HIMALAYAN BIODIVERSITY TRAINING INSTITUTE, SIKKIM

THE BUTTERFLY RESERVE, SIKKIM

MANORI CREEK, MARVE

MY MUMBAI
ROBERT VERRIJT

MUMBAI IS SPECIAL BECAUSE
It has many worlds and centuries in one.

THIS CAN BE IMPROVED
Every single building built in the past half a century except *Kanchanjunga Apartments*, designed by Charles Correa and located on Cumballa Hill. It is the only building that has been designed for Indian people and Indian climatic conditions. It has taken the 'bungalow in the sky' concept and realized it. It has not made the occupant dependant on living in a closed air-conditioned box. It is only now again that the concepts of verandas is being reintroduced in high rise apartment buildings.

MY FAVOURITE PLACE
Our terrace at home.

MY FAVOURITE RESTAURANT
The favourite places keep changing so fast... However *Britannia* [*Britannia & Company Restaurant*], the Parsi cafe in Ballard Estate remains on our list for its delicious *berry pulao* and *sali botti* [mutton cooked in a tomato onion gravy and garnished with deep-fried potatoes]. *The Dome* at Marine Drive is nice too, for the view it offers of the city. And *Indigo Deli* for being one of the first of its kind and continuing to serve delicious food in Mumbai.

THE BEST PLACE TO RELAX
Anywhere outside Mumbai. Particularly Alibaug is great for its proximity to the city and the feel of Goa that it brings so close to home.

IF ONE THING COULD BE DEMOLISHED IT WOULD BE
Mr. Ambani's high-rise villa called *Antilia*. It is a 27-floor personal home. He could have made something that benefits society as well, you know, the way John Rockefeller built the *Rockefeller Center*. He could have used the bottom five stories for a public swimming pool, a museum...

MY CHOICE OF TRANSPORTATION
The car, until we get the NS [Dutch Railways] trains in Mumbai.

MY FAVOURITE LANDMARK
That would be *Marine Lines' Art Deco district*. Why? For the potential it holds – with a better upkeep – to lend the city a face. It can be a genuine landmark and give the city a true international character. With the beautiful backdrop of Art Deco buildings, the Marine Drive promenade lit up at night to form the 'Queen's Necklace', the Chowpatty beach on one side and South Mumbai's business district on the other... All in all it is a great example of urban design.

MY FAVOURITE MUMBAI BOOK
Midnight's Children (1980) by Salman Rushdie.

MY FAVOURITE MUMBAI FILM
Slumdog Millionaire (2008), for being the first movie to finally show the vibrancy – but also the rough side of the city – in such a joyful and non-moralizing way.

IF NOT MUMBAI THEN
Of all Indian cities it is Mumbai only...

WHAT WE CAN LEARN FROM MUMBAI
We can learn from the entrepreneurship of its people.

FROM QUANTITY TO QUALITY

RAVI SARANGAN

Ravi Sarangan (1965) completed a Bachelor's degree programme in Architecture in 1987 at Sir J.J. College of Architecture in Mumbai. Together with Sanjay Srinivasan, soon after graduation he founded *Edifice Consultants*. Presently he is director, with a focus on business development and brand & knowledge management.

With 225 employees and a direct presence in seven cities in India, *Edifice* works across all sectors in the fields of master planning, architectural and interior design. They undertake residential, educational, hospitality, health, retail and commercial projects. Their portfolio includes campuses and headquarters for some of India's largest companies, such as *Tata Consultancy Services* and *Infosys Technologies*, as well as for major global clients such as *Goldman Sachs, Vodafone, Deutsche Bank* and *Holiday Inn*. In 2010, the magazine *Construction World* listed *Edifice* among *India's Top 10 Architects*. A year later the magazine *Architects & Interiors* mentioned *Edifice* as 'one of the 50 most prominent and fabulous architects of India'.

'He is our hero', Ravi Sarangan says, nodding towards the image of Mahatma Gandhi on the wall in the meeting room. 'When you ask our costumers about *Edifice* in the market, there is one word that you will hear: trust. We focus on values. Trust, integrity, ethics. These are at the core of our work ethic.'

The glass doors in the office are lettered with texts emphasizing these values. The texts and the picture of Gandhi are not just decorations, or some fancy, Ravi emphasizes. They are at the core of what *Edifice* wants to stand for. But it was not always like that.

BEGINNINGS

Upon graduation from the Sir J.J. College of Architecture in 1987, Sanjay Srinivasan and Ravi Sarangan decided to start their own firm. 'At that time it was fashionable to start something by yourself. Unlike the present, when most graduates prefer to join an existing firm.' The classmates set up shop in a small garage in Chembur. 'It's not an exaggeration to say small: it was sixteen by eight feet [5 by 2.5 metres]!', Ravi laughs.

Twenty five years later it is hard to imagine those humble beginnings. The company grew exponentially. At its peak, some seven years ago, *Edifice* had 300 employees (at present there are 225). The humble garage has been replaced by seven offices in as many cities: *Edifice* is present in Mumbai, Bengaluru, Pune, Kolkata, Chennai, Hyderabad and New Delhi. Mumbai and Bengaluru host their design studios. The offices in the other cities focus on project execution.

Edifice burgeoned on the waves of the economic boom starting in the mid-1990s. Their first projects consisted mostly of refurbishments of office buildings occupied by IT and technology firms. As these companies grew bigger, and new firms opened offices, so did *Edifice*. *Infosys, Tata Consultancy Services, Cognizant Technologies, Syntel, Cipla, Apollo Hospitals, Dow Chemicals, Vodafone, Bennett & Coleman*... the list of companies they designed grand office buildings for seems endless. Over the years they worked in almost every perceivable sector: corporate buildings, urban design, hospitality, education, health care, and large residential and commercial buildings all found a place in their portfolio. For a long time, *Edifice* was like so many other firms: focused on quantity and size rather than quality, working to generate money rather than acclaim. Until the economy slowed down in October 2008.

FROM DESIGN FACTORY TO DESIGN HOUSE

When the recession hit, the directors decided to focus on design quality and to reduce the number of projects they would take on. 'We felt it was the right time to make major changes in our firm', Ravi remembers. 'We were seen as experts in delivering projects, but not as great designers. Our aim was to be proud of every project we design. We still want to reach our commercial targets, but we also want acclaim, win accolades and awards, and get our work published, for example.'

'From a design factory we became a design house', Ravi says. 'The result is that people are now taking *Edifice* very seriously in terms of design. Earlier we were collaborating with international firms. Now we are competing with them!', he adds with pride.

To illustrate the turnaround of the company, Ravi sums up their success at competitions of late. 'These are the litmus test for quality architecture', he feels. 'In 2009 we competed for the World Architecture News Awards (WAN) in Commercial-Unbuild category with a design for the headquarters of Anil Ambani's *Reliance Energy*. We came in the top six of the world. After that we competed for the new head office of the Income Tax Department in New Delhi. We stood fifth. Then followed IIT [Indian Institute of Technology] Jodhpur. Our design was the runner up. And the last competition we entered in was for the IIM [Indian Institute of Management] in Udaipur. We will hear the result later this month.' Winning this last competition would mean that *Edifice* 'has arrived', Ravi feels. 'Louis Kahn did IIM Ahmedabad and BV Doshi did his IIM in Bengaluru... So, yes, in India, when you get that assignment, when you get to do an IIM or an IIT, you have definitely reached the highest echelons.'

GREEN BUILDING

Edifice has a strong thrust towards sustainable and environment friendly – or green – design. Ravi explains: 'In all our work we keep the climate in mind. In fact, working in as vast a country as India means that you work for five major climates. You have the cold climate in the Northern part of India, with mean monthly temperatures of less than 25 degrees Celsius. But there is also the hot and dry zone of Rajasthan and Central India where the humidity is relatively low, but the mean monthly temperature is over 30 degrees Celsius. Then there are temperate areas such as Pune and Bengaluru [with temperatures generally ranging between 25 and 30 degrees], and warm and humid regions such as Mumbai and Chennai. Finally, there are composite areas, where six months of the year they do not fall into any of the categories; New Delhi is a good example of this. Each of these zones requires different solutions.'

Ravi feels that attention for green building has come just in time. 'I am not a big fan of those certifying bodies that are being established, as I think their focus is too limited. But at the same time it is good that it *is* happening now in India. We were on the wrong track before. We were going the China and Middle East way with all those glass boxes. At *Edifice* we follow the GRIHA [Green Rating for Integrated Habitat Assessment] developed by TERI [The Energy and Resource Institute, New Delhi] and the Ministry of New and Renewable Energy, although there are projects of ours going in for the LEED [Leadership in Energy and Environmental Design] rating as well.'

INDIAN ARCHITECTURE

Edifice applies new and traditional solutions for sustainability in their buildings. 'Take our building for *Tata Consultancy Services* in Hyderabad', Ravi says. ' It is a contemporary structure, but based on some traditional Indian architecture ideas. The materials for the building were sourced locally. The walls are thick for passive cooling. Natural light comes in from the corridors, which have a north-facing light opening on the roof. There is glazing, but only on the northern side. The west and the south walls are dead. This way we managed to make the air-conditioning load only half of what it normally is for a building this size'.

Whether or not his architecture is Indian, is a difficult question, Ravi finds. 'Our vision is that our designs should be sensitive to the context, the climate, and the client. These are our three C's. But I hate to contribute a particular nametag to it. As long as a solution is contextual, if it suits the climate where it will be build, is sensitive to the client's function and desire, and if you can source materials for it in a 150-kilometre radius, than to me, the building is Indian. Or Indian enough. It may not look and feel traditional, but in terms of materials and suitability for the climate, yes, our buildings are Indian.'

INTEGRITY

'*Edifice* holds integrity at the centre of its business philosophy and work practice', says Ravi. 'We started off as a "clean company', striving to put an end to corruption, to work ethically, and on a basis of trust.' They put posters up at the entrance informing contractors, vendors and others that they would not accept any gifts and favours. 'Initially we were commanding a low fee to gain entry into the market. This we did until 2008. Then we started asking a higher fee for our work. Confronted with our new policy, clients would ask us: "Why do you ask such a high fee, when I know you get kickbacks from the contractor and vendors?" We would tell them straight: "We don't. We only work for a fee. Go ask the vendors. They know about us."'

Ravi admits it was a risky move to start with a clean slate. 'People started writing our obituaries already. And some clients stopped working with us. But that is fine. In fact, we told them: "If you want to work in that way, than don't approach us any more". We proved everyone wrong. We have plenty of work now', Ravi says.

FRATERNITY

For Ravi it is not enough that his own company is 'clean'. His aim is bigger than that. He wants to see societal change happen. The *Edifice* office remained closed the day anti-corruption activist Anna Hazare brought his campaign to Mumbai in 2011. 'All employees joined us to Azad Maidan and the Bandra & Juhu walk, where Anna Hazare held his protest, to support his cause.' And Ravi wants to see change among other architects as well. 'I want our sector and profession to become noble again', he says. 'Somewhere we all share responsibility for the disintegration of the system. So what I have done is to take the initiative to call big architects to get together and cleanse the system.'

At present there is no overarching network, no platform or body to which architects can associate to meet each other for exchange. 'If you want to meet the fraternity you basically rely on vendors who organize cocktail parties. Those are the only occasions we meet. It shouldn't be like that.' He is working on setting up a body from where he can push for reforms.

TCS THANE, YANTRA PARK, THANE

VODAFONE INDIA HEADQUARTERS, PENINSULA CORPORATE PARK, PAREL, MUMBAI

DADAR WEST

MY MUMBAI
RAVI SARANGAN

MUMBAI IS SPECIAL BECAUSE
It is a very inclusive city. It gives anyone and everyone an opportunity to be part of it. You, me, the *rickshaw-wallah*, the city cuts across social strata.

THIS CAN BE IMPROVED
Sanitation and public transport. I read about a survey recently that was done by the municipality on toilets in the city. They found that over a million slum dwellers in this city have no toilet facilities on their premises and defecate in the open. Those who do have access to a toilet in their slum often have to share it with a large number of people. The ratio is something like eighty people for one toilet. And in some areas it is much worse than that.

MY FAVOURITE RESTAURANT
Govinda on Babulnath Road and *Crystal*, near Wilson College. Both are near Chowpatty Beach and both have great vegetarian food.

MY FAVOURITE LANDMARK
Marine Drive, the three-kilometre long boulevard in South Mumbai. The street and the promenade along it follow the bay, which is C-shaped. The buildings on Marine Drive were built in the 1920s and 1930s in the Art Deco style. Only Miami, USA, has more Art Deco buildings along the sea-front than Mumbai has.

THE BEST PLACE TO RELAX
My home.

IF ONE THING COULD BE DEMOLISHED IT WOULD BE
I would like to demolish structures that have come up on our *maidans* [open grounds]. I really hate it when slums, political rallies and private development encroach into already limited public spaces and grounds.

MY CHOICE OF TRANSPORTATION
If not my own car, than a *Meru Cab* or a *Tab Cab*, taxi's you can call in advance.

WITH UNLIMITED FREEDOM AND MONEY TO DO WHATEVER I WANT IN MUMBAI, I WOULD
Clean it up. I think it is just a matter of doing it again and again. Dirt attracts dirt, and if places are kept clean people are less likely to throw waste there.

IF NOT MUMBAI THEN
Anywhere in India. If a guy can stay in Mumbai, he can live anywhere else!

WHAT WE CAN LEARN FROM MUMBAI
Resilience.

ACKNOWLEDGEMENTS

The *Learning from Mumbai* project began in September 2010 in Mumbai, when Gert Jan Scholte met the Principal of Sir J.J. College of Architecture, Rajiv Mishra, who subsequently invited us to come give a workshop. His enthusiasm, in addition to the opportunity to revisit the city where we had studied twenty years ago, were the impetus to start making plans. We wanted to return to the city to rediscover it.

Although our goal was clear, the way to reach it was much less so. We wanted to put together a positive book, providing a number of perspectives. The interview format we chose made it possible to literally give the floor to inspired architects and urban planners. Every single conversation thus became another special introduction to Mumbai.

In April 2012, when we were on the verge of conducting the interviews, we were lucky to run into Sanne Vanderkaaij Gandhi. From that moment on, we collaborated with Sanne on the book. Our second trip to Mumbai was in June. Interviews, workshops and lectures added up to a very intensive programme.

In early December we travelled to Mumbai for the third time, to dot the i's and cross the t's. This trip, too, turned out to have a pleasant surprise in store for us, when we made the acquaintance of photographer Bas Losekoot. His photographs are a means of observing Mumbai closely.

In addition to Rajiv Mishra, Sanne Vanderkaaij Gandhi and Bas Losekoot, we want to extend our gratitude to the authors of the reflective articles: Rohan Varma, Charles Correa and Rahul Mehrotra. We are also very grateful to the architects, urban planners and other professionals who allowed us to interview them: Nitya Amarnath, Shefali Balwani, Steven Beunder, Hafeez Contractor, PK Das, Arun Deodhar, Saloni Deodhar, Sushma Deodhar, Kartik Gala, Shyam Khandekar, Sapna Lakhe, Abhijit Mandrekar, Chaitanya Modak, Dhanya Pilo, Ravi Sarangan, Shazeb Shaikh, Shwetambari Shinde, Brinda Somaya, Adrienne Thadani and Robert Verrijt. We further warmly thank for their help and support: the staff and students of the Sir J.J. College of Architecture, Nicola Antaki (*Fresh & Local*), Marijke van Drunen Littel, Marthe Lamers, Celiza Peters and Ila Singh (*Consulate General of the Kingdom of the Netherlands*), Anne Feenstra (*arch i*), Anuradha Gupta (*Dutch DFA*), Nishant Gupta (*Architect Hafeez Contractor*), Nazanin Hedayati and Martijn Oskam (*Creative Industries Fund NL*), Bipin Shah (Mapin Publishing), Robert Stephens (*RMA Architects*), Sunay Gandhi, Georgina Grant, Eloise Sky Scholte and Merel Smit. Last, but certainly not least, we want to warmly thank our editor David Raats and our graphic designer Ilse van Klei.

Pelle Poiesz and Gert Jan Scholte

VIEW FROM AMARSONS GARDEN

White Flowers

DADAR RAILWAY STATION